"*Unapologetic* is about tapping into who you really are and the unique gifts you bring to the world. In *Unapologetic*, you'll learn how to connect with your brilliance and essence so you can shine your bright light in an unapologetic way."

~Christy Whitman,

New York Times Bestselling author

"Tammy's new book, *Unapologetic*, is a powerful journey into why we apologize. This is going to be your trusted handbook as you explore, get curious and reframe your mindset so you can show up in your life authentically and Unapologetically!!!"

~Dawn Duffy,

Intuitive Energy Healer

"As a life coaching client of Tammy's for three years now, I have experienced firsthand the power in Tammy's message to stop apologizing for yourself and to stand in your power. I am so excited that the world gets to experience this now! Reading *Unapologetic* feels like having a true, raw and liberating conversation with an old friend. Tammy's personal stories and self-guided exercises help the reader turn words into actions, making this a powerful, moving read that is sure to change your life if you let it."

~Miranda Rodriguez,

Marketing Coach

"Unapologetic teaches you how to unleash the beautiful power within you to live an intentional life that you truly love!"

~**Karen Putz,**

Author of Unwrapping Your Passion

"How many times did you apologize today?" Tammy's book starts with that simple question, but it's a powerful one that stopped me dead in my tracks before I'd even made it to Chapter 1. Tammy has created something special here and her words made me question my own approach to my dreams, goals and aspirations."

~**Jon Acuff,**

New York Times Bestselling author of *Soundtracks, the Surprising Solution to Overthinking*

"Like a trusted friend, Tammy holds out her hand to carefully and gracefully walk with the reader on the road of discovery, intention, and acceptance. Her words are infused with well-watered wisdom that offers focus and clarity. This is no traditional self-help book; rather, it is a trusted guide for lasting change."

~**Ronne Rock,**

Mentor and author of *One Woman Can Change the World: Reclaiming Your God-Designed Influence and Impact Right Where You Are*

"Tammy Helfrich has written a must read for anyone embarking on the journey of self discovery. *Unapologetic* is full of wisdom, personal stories, & questions that speak directly to the heart of the seeker that is searching for their purpose in life."

~ **Sheri Strzelecki,**

Life Coach & Wellness Practitioner at Centered Soul Space

"In *Unapologetic* Tammy makes such great points - why are we out here apologizing all day everyday?! To find the answer to that question she guides you, step by step, like she's right there with you all the way."

Kelsey Humphreys,

Author and musical comedian @*TheKelseyShow*

"I met Tammy at that fateful conference in 2011, and her personal journey has been inspiring. And now she's calling us to join her. *Unapologetic* confronts a culture that's taught so many people to hide our superpowers, to adapt and defer to others, and to be ashamed of our unique Awesome. These lies are not only toxic to us as individuals, but they rob the greater community of our best contributions. *Unapologetic* is a call to arms—to embrace our individual superpowers and to share them with confidence and power."

Chris Niles,

Author of the Shark Key Adventure Series

UNAPOLOGETIC

STAND IN YOUR POWER

TAMMY HELFRICH

ALSO BY TAMMY HELFRICH

Becoming a LifeChanger: Move Away from Ordinary

Right Where You Are Encouragement Journal

Intention Journal

TAMMY HELFRICH COACHING LLC

Copyright 2021 by Tammy Helfrich Coaching LLC

All rights reserved.

ISBN: 9798530760716

For Rick, Jonah, and Kaden.

You've taught me the most about learning to be unapologetically me. Your love, support, and guidance mean the world to me. Here's to many more adventures in this beautiful life we've been given.

CONTENTS

PROLOGUE

As I was being wheeled into emergency surgery for a ruptured ectopic pregnancy, my doctor was not happy with me. He insisted on knowing why I had not been clearer with the emergency room physician about how serious of a situation I was in. So what did I do? I apologized to him. I was alone and crying and apologizing to a doctor for the actions of an ER doctor who refused to listen to me explain what little I knew of my situation. I'm so grateful that this frightening experience turned out okay, as I only understood after the fact that the surgery saved my life.

Reflecting on this experience not only brings up gratitude. It also brings up frustration and anger. I apologized, for something I didn't know much about and for someone else's actions and unwillingness to listen. This is an extreme example, but I think we can relate to this in so many ways in our daily lives. We apologize a lot. We take on the responsibility to apologize for, not only ourselves, but others as well. And it simply is not helpful most of the time.

As a life coach, I have practiced learning to understand myself and to be aware of the sneaky thoughts and ways that we are not always kind and loving to ourselves. I help clients learn to understand this as well and practice knowing themselves better. I wrote this book because I continually hear people apologizing for who they are. It is always hard to hear, as I have spent years working on this for myself. We are all created by the same creator, and the idea that we are required to apologize for ourselves is not inherent in our nature. It's learned. The good news is that it can be unlearned.

My two boys have helped me to understand this in a way that has been so helpful for me. They were uniquely wired from the minute they made their appearance on this earth, and it has been an honor to raise them and help them understand themselves. I want to help you do the same. I believe you have amazing gifts to bring to the world. I call it bringing your awesome to the world. But this often isn't encouraged because we've been taught and told for most of our lives that there are specific ways to do things and ways that we should behave. And if you don't fit into those molds, then that means there is something wrong with you. I simply no longer believe that is true.

This book is about helping you learn to understand yourself better and to tap into the uniqueness that makes you - YOU! And more importantly, to stop apologizing for it. To learn to be yourself and bring your gifts to the world in a way that is honoring, loving, and gives others the permission to do the same.

My desire is that you will take however long you need with this book to truly let it sink in.

Feel free to answer questions, journal, and write about what comes up for you as you read. If you have found yourself apologizing for strengths or weaknesses or simply for everything you do, then I hope you will find some comfort and encouragement in the pages ahead. I often remind my clients that I don't have their answers. They do. So, I want to tell you that as well. While you will find encouragement and ideas to consider in this book, you are the only one who lives your life and knows what resonates with you and what you are willing to work on. Be open and curious about what this book brings up for you.

I'm so excited that you are here and hope that it will feel as if we are sitting down and having a great cup of coffee together. Well, actually, I would be drinking a chai. But you get the idea. I hope it feels like we are looking each other in the eye and sharing our journeys together. Learning to be unapologetic starts with a safe space, and I hope this book will be that for you. I have learned to be unapologetic and you can, too. All you need to do is get honest with yourself and be open and curious.

Here's to the journey of exploring YOU!

~ Tammy

INTRODUCTION

How many times did you apologize today?

Do you have any idea?

Or has it become so natural and so ingrained that you admit you apologize for everything?

Maybe you apologized for what you said to someone this morning at work. Maybe you apologized for not being fully present in a meeting. Maybe you apologized for wearing something someone else didn't like. Maybe you apologized for talking to someone your friend didn't want you to talk to. Maybe you apologized for setting boundaries by saying no, but someone was unhappy about that. Maybe you apologized for being yourself, simply because someone else told you that you should.

From the time we are young, we are told what to do and to apologize if we don't do it exactly how someone tells us we should. This leads us to learn to apologize for ourselves. Over and over again. We apologize because we are not doing it the way someone else thinks we should. We learn how to apologize for who we are. And we can live our entire lives doing this.

I have asked many people what they find themselves apologizing for, and the most common answer by far was "everything." Whoa.

Why do we feel like we have to apologize for everything in our lives? Where does that come from, and why are we okay with it?

Apologizing is defined by Oxford Languages as expressing regret or remorse for actions. In essence, we have regret and remorse for who we are. And it is toxic.

We are not born like this. If you've ever had a child or met a child, you know that kids are very rarely apologetic. We have to train them to learn to apologize. They are who they are, and they don't care what anyone else thinks about it! They are relentless in the pursuit of what they want, and they are completely comfortable with who they are.

So, isn't it interesting that, as we grow older, we completely tame this unapologetic part of ourselves and often go in the other direction? We learn to apologize for everything and for who we are. And we don't even realize it. We don't understand the impact that it is having on us as individuals and as a collective society. We often forget that we are uniquely wired because we've been conditioned to try to be like everyone else. When in reality, what works for me often doesn't work well for you, and that's totally okay. But we don't realize this and end up learning to apologize for who we are and how we show up in the world. We neglect ourselves and don't do what we want to do, which often leads to asking for permission to be ourselves.

The truth is that we don't actually need permission to be ourselves. But most of us think we do. I remember being at a conference with Jon Acuff and hearing stories about people working towards their dreams and learning to accept themselves for who they are and being uniquely themselves. And it moved me deeply. At the end of that conference, Jon gave a very moving talk that had me in tears. He said, "Your dream matters. The world needs you to do it." Not only was he being unapologetic about who he was and what he was offering to the world, but he was essentially giving me permission to start thinking differently and to begin this journey of learning to understand myself in a completely new way. All because he had done the same and was following his passion to tell others about it.

That conference was in 2011. I had been on my journey for a while at that point, but I had two young boys, a full-time stressful corporate career, and a marriage that had been up and down for several years. I was waking up to the idea that there could be more to the life I was living. It was both frightening and exhilarating at the same time. My journey to becoming unapologetic has taken quite a few years. It hasn't been easy, but it has absolutely been worth it.

In this book, I will share stories, experiences, and tools that have helped me learn to know myself better, remember who I am, and learn to live with abundance and strength. Unapologetic is not about being a jerk and not caring about others. In fact, it's the exact opposite. It is about learning to love and honor yourself and live authentically as you, which is one of the most caring things you can do for yourself and those you love and care about. It is available to you, and you can start today.

I look forward to guiding you on this journey. I'd encourage you to have a pen and journal handy, as I will be asking you questions and prompt you to think about your life. You can go through this book at whatever pace works for you. I'd love for you to do more than just read this book. It may mean that you take action on what you read. Or it may mean that you simply choose to look at your life in a very honest way for the first time. You always get to decide what works best for you. However, my wish is that you will choose to do something more than just consume this content. Learning to integrate what we learn is where true change happens.

I want to guide you and help you, but your journey is your own. Set an intention that this book is about YOU. It's about you learning how to understand yourself better and to move towards being unapologetic, in whatever way that resonates with you.

Are you ready? Here we go.

CHAPTER ONE

WHY DO WE APOLOGIZE?

In 2014, I left a successful corporate career in sales after an 18+ year career. I had climbed the corporate ladder, gotten promotions, worked for a Fortune 500 company, and did "all the things" that everyone tells you to do in your career. But I was not fulfilled. I was stressed, overworked, and on the verge of adrenal failure. It was no way to live. I did not leave hastily. In fact, my husband and I had been strategically planning for me to make a move for almost two years. And we both knew it was the right move.

But do you know what I found myself doing? Apologizing!

Over and over again. To my bosses, to my colleagues, and to my family who could not comprehend why I would make such a move. I apologized for making a decision that I knew was right for me. It didn't stop me from making the move and not looking back, but I often wonder what it would have felt like to be fully and completely me and never apologize to anyone for my decision.

It's important to state that I'm not talking about not apologizing when we have done something wrong. I'm talking about the sneaky ways that we apologize for who we are, what we like, and who we want to be in the world. That has been my work for the last several years: to learn to know myself in a way that releases the shame and guilt and reasons why I apologize. To learn to be totally okay with an unapologetic me. This takes lots of practice, and life coaching has been the biggest help to me in learning to do this. It's also why I chose to become a life coach. To help others learn to understand themselves and be aligned with their core desires and design. It is a gift and an honor to walk alongside others as they learn to know and accept themselves for who they are and stop apologizing for it.

I think there are multiple reasons why we apologize. Many of us have been conditioned to think that we are broken. That there is something wrong with us and that we need to apologize because we aren't perfect. I don't mean to burst your bubble, but there is no such thing as perfect. Oh, we think there is, but there really isn't. Your version of perfect is different than mine, and we can all disagree about the specifics. Therefore, we are continually striving for something that isn't even real.

We think that if we just fix ourselves and be better then everything will be okay.

And we will actually like ourselves. What if you are not broken at all? What if there is nothing wrong with you and you are an amazing human, but you've just forgotten it? What would that mean for you?

I had to do a lot of work around this idea. Growing up in a very conservative Christian environment, it was drilled into my head that I was broken and not worthy. Looking back, I can see that I never truly believed that in my soul, but those messages were really strong. If you grew up with a similar background, maybe you can relate. It wasn't until the last decade of my life that I have come to believe that simply isn't true. We are created by an amazing creator and our starting point is good. If you have ever had a baby or looked at a brand new baby, it's hard to argue with this. They are not broken or awful from the time they enter this world, they are pure and innocent. I know this can take some time to remember, but if you truly sit and think about it, you can start to believe it too.

We also become conditioned to forget who we are. We get caught up in life and circumstances, and we forget who we are at our core. We forget what we like, what we don't like, and we learn to play a game where we wear lots of masks. We learn to be what other people tell us to be or what we think they want us to be. It's conditioning that many of us experience throughout our lives without even realizing it. It isn't always bad. In fact, we need to do some of this early in our life to start to figure out who we are. When we first go into adulthood and start to see who we are outside of our parents, we often quickly fit into roles that seem okay to us. And we can stay there for our entire lives if we choose.

The challenge can be when we are living someone else's story or idea of life instead of our own. When we are doing what we think we "should" instead of what we really want to do.

We can all fake it for quite a while, but sooner or later, it seems to catch up with us.

We look around and wonder what happened to the person we were and why we seem so unhappy all the time. All of these situations are why we learn to start apologizing for who we are. Because somewhere deep down we know that we aren't living into who we've been created to be. We know there's a disconnect, but we just can't seem to find it.

So it's easier to just apologize for everything and keep ourselves stuck in this cycle. The list of "I'm sorry" phrases could take up the entirety of this book.

Allow yourself to dream about what a difference it would make and consider your answers to these questions.

What if you didn't need to apologize anymore simply for being you?

What if you could live your life unapologetically and feel great about it?

What would be different in your life?

How would you show up differently?

What would being unapologetic mean to you?

Notes

CHAPTER TWO

INTERRUPT NORMAL

I really started to understand the power of learning to stop apologizing as I embarked on my own spiritual journey. As I mentioned, I grew up in a very conservative Christian environment. And I am grateful for the lessons and the teachings I learned. But something always felt off for me. So I walked away from the church for a while in my early 20's and 30's. I just couldn't seem to find a church that fit with what I believed and just knew to be true deep in my soul.

As we started our family, I knew that understanding my own faith and what I believed was important for me so that I could help my children learn this as well. This led me on an adventure to explore my own faith, what I really believed and no longer believed, and how I could incorporate this into my life in a deeper way. This was not easy work, as it required questioning so many things I had been told to believe and systems of religion that I had just come to accept. What I came to understand is that my relationship with my creator was my own, and it wasn't confined to a church or a religion or a doctrine. Yes, those things can be incredibly important on your journey, as they were on my own journey, but they aren't the prerequisite. A relationship with our creator is available to each and every one of us, simply by being willing to explore and opening ourselves up to the divine.

This was the start of my journey to understand myself better. When I could fully accept that I was made in the image of my creator and I did not have to fix myself in order to be unconditionally loved, that broke something open inside of me. It allowed me to see that maybe I no longer had to wear the masks of what other people expected me to be. Maybe I could embrace who I was and start to explore what that looked like. This was not an overnight process. This took time and experimenting and starting to ask myself questions about what I really liked and what I didn't. And learning to be okay with the uneasy feeling in the process. I remember my pastor stating that "we can't separate our emotional health from our spiritual health." Something about that statement really resonated with me. I had been so segmented and compartmentalized in my experiences, that I thought you could just work on one of them and it would all be fine. While you may need to work on one at a time, it is important to know that they are interconnected. We are energetic beings and our physical, mental, spiritual, and emotional health are all interconnected, whether we can see it or not.

Learning to ask myself these questions slowly woke me up to my life. I had been sleepwalking and just going through the motions for quite a while. I was extremely comfortable in our life and my work and just existing in many ways. When I looked at my life, by all outside appearances, it was really good. But there was a disconnect and a longing for something more. Something deeper that had meaning and could help me tap into my strengths and gifts and learn how to share them with the world.

On this journey, I started writing again. It was something that I had loved to do as a teen but had not really done much of as I got older. People had often told me that my thoughts were very well put together and I used writing in my business life, but I had not considered sharing my thoughts with the world. Part of my waking up process involved starting to share my thoughts in written form through blogging, and it completely opened me up in a way that I hadn't expected. We often forget about the things we loved to do in our youth. I had completely forgotten how much I liked to write poems and stories and letters to friends. Picking this up again was so helpful as I learned to express myself in new ways.

I had spent most of my adult life in a very structured, corporate environment and had learned how to play the game very well. But on this journey, I realized that this environment just wasn't working for me anymore. I couldn't pinpoint it at the time, but I can now look back and see that it was because I had been suppressing my entrepreneurial spirit for most of my life. My dad was an entrepreneur, as were my uncles and multiple people within our family and friend circle. I chose to explore a career in the corporate world because it felt safer to me at that time, and I don't regret it. But waking up to the idea that there might be something else out there for me was incredibly helpful and scary and exciting.

During this time, I was also watching as my good friend Jamie was fighting cancer and living her bucket list in her early 30's. She was beautiful and full of life, and our kids were born one day apart. Watching her experience cancer and sharing her experiences with all of us woke me up to my own life and the fragility of it. If this could happen to her, a seemingly healthy and vibrant young woman, it could happen to any of us. It was so challenging to watch, but also woke me up to my own humanity and pushed me to ask myself how I was really living. Was I? Or was I just existing? She documented her journey on her blog, which I was able to publish in a book titled *Much Love from Jamie* in 2017. The proceeds of the book benefit Jamie's Wish Foundation, which her friends started in her honor after her death.

Life is short, friends. We are only here for a limited amount of time.

Jamie and so many others reminded me that it was time to start living and to enjoy life in a way that I hadn't for quite a few years. It was time to start understanding who I was, what I had to offer the world, and to live in a way that felt more aligned with who I was at my core. This journey took time for me, and it will take time for you, too. But I would not change one bit of it, as it has helped me become who I am today.

Consider these questions for yourself:

Where could you interrupt normal?

Where in your life are you completely comfortable even though you may not want to be?

What could interrupting normal look like for you?

Be super curious about this and spend some time writing about it.

Notes

CHAPTER THREE

HOW DO WE DO THIS?

So, how do we start the process of interrupting normal and thinking about our lives differently? For me, it started with opening myself up to new voices. I've always been a big reader and have had a love for self-development since I discovered it in college. I had a Marketing professor, shoutout to Dr. Rick Ridnour, who was an amazingly energetic and engaging speaker. I saw something in him that I wanted. An energy, a philosophy about life, and a presence that was warm and engaging and full of life. He encouraged us to start reading self-help and self-development books, including his own that he had written called *Mental Vitamins*. I still have a copy of it to this day and am grateful for his influence.

There has always been a draw to learn about new ideas and opportunities for growth. I now understand that it's because when I recognize those amazing qualities in others, it's because they are also available to me. They are qualities in me, too. Anytime we see something in someone else, we can recognize that it is also available to us. Many teachers have talked about the idea of how we exist to be mirrors to each other. What we see in others is a direct reflection of ourselves, both in the good and not so great ways. I think that's why self-development has always been important to me. I knew there was something more and I wanted to learn and absorb as much of it as I could. But, as it often happens in our lives, I stopped reading books for a while and got caught up in life. So when I embarked on the journey of getting to know myself better, I decided to start reading some new authors and open myself up to new perspectives.

Authors like Jon Acuff, Bob Goff, Brene Brown, Anne Lamott, and so many others became the people I was reading and listening to. People who were living a life that was intriguing to me. I was starting to write again, so that was also helpful, but they were instrumental in opening my eyes up to new ideas and thoughts. Looking back now, I can see that it was drawing me to consider options I had never thought of before. I also started talking to people in my community. Entrepreneurs, creatives, writers, and people who were not in the traditional corporate world. I started a series on my blog titled "Life-Changers" to highlight them and even wrote an ebook about some of them. It's called *Becoming a LifeChanger: Move Away from Ordinary* and you can find it on Amazon. The book had good reviews and it was so fun to create something I had never created before.

"People who live inspiring lives motivate me. There is something incredibly energizing about their presence. I love hearing about their dreams, passions, and even the obstacles they have overcome because that is often where the inspiration started. In the details of their stories. Life changing stories.

*I call these people **LifeChangers**."*

After writing that book, I had a friend confront me with a powerful truth. In that ebook, I did not write anything about myself as an example of a LifeChanger. The truth is, I didn't think I was at that time. I didn't think I had anything interesting to contribute, as I was still living the normal, traditional life in the corporate world. Other than writing, I didn't think I was living outside of ordinary. That was a very powerful revelation for me, as so much of this journey was about learning to understand myself better and choose my own path moving forward.

That awareness led me on a path to some of the deepest personal work I have ever done in my life. I eventually left my corporate career, continued to write and blog, and started a podcast called *Right Where You Are*, where I interviewed authors and creatives and people living outside of ordinary. I also chose to leave the corporate career and embark on a brand new journey with a nonprofit, where I learned an entirely new way of working with creative teams and individuals on their personal journeys. It was both liberating and challenging to learn something so different.

One of the biggest benefits of this career move was working in a creative team that was also very close and personal. This allowed me to feel seen in a way that I never had in the corporate world. We not only worked together, but we also were growing and expanding and doing our own work. Let me tell you that while that sounds amazing, it is hard and can be really messy work. We all have our issues and challenges and being able to talk about them openly is freeing, but also can be very difficult sometimes. I do not regret any of the work, though, as it has helped me to see myself in ways that I could never have imagined. One of the things I truly believe we all want is to be seen and heard. Challenging myself to be in this environment was a way of allowing myself to be seen and heard in a new way. It also challenged me to learn to know myself better so that I could begin to open up to new ideas and be more vulnerable, and also learn how to see others in a new and deeper way.

I approached this journey to understand myself better as an experiment. I knew I would have to try many different things in order to start to know myself well and learn how to finally accept myself for who I was. I experimented with therapy, yoga, the Enneagram, energy work, coaching, fitness, spiritual direction, conferences, getting to know authors and creatives, and reading and following many people talking about personal development and growth. It was a fascinating time consuming massive amounts of information. I joined book launch teams, guest posted on blogs, interviewed people for my podcast, and continued writing. Basically, I was on the search for the answer to Tammy. Who was she and what did she want? And what would it take to get to where I wanted to go? Could I ever figure out what I actually wanted?

While I am grateful for this journey, I can now see that I truly believed someone else had my answers. I thought that the next guru or class would finally tell me the missing piece of how to fix ME! We've been trained this way from the time we are very little. There's something wrong with us. We're broken and need to be fixed. Or someone else knows better than we do what is best for us. This is not the case at all when we are younger. We know what we want and we are not afraid to ask for it. And we don't believe anyone else knows better than we do. So how do we get ourselves wrapped up in looking outside of ourselves? If you're feeling your heart beat a little faster right now, know that you are not alone. It is so normal for all of us to think that we should know the answer or that if we just keep searching, we will eventually stumble upon it. But in my own quest, the missing piece I was looking for was always ME! Always. Sure, I learned things from people and implemented suggestions that they had, but at the end of the day, my answers and what works for me is what I was searching for.

I am grateful for the time I spent experimenting and learning more about myself. I learned a lot of things about myself that I never knew. I started to really question the persona and the way that I showed up in the world. I started to wonder if who I thought I was for all of my life was really me. I tried new things, pushed myself outside of my comfort zone, met people I would have never expected, and gave myself grace during the process.

As I did this, I started to remember who I was in my past. For example, near the end of high school, I decided that I wanted to choose a career in business. I wanted what I believed to be the "safe" route where I could work for a corporation and make good money and keep climbing the corporate ladder. After watching my mom have to go into the workforce in her 50's, this seemed like a great way to never have to do that. I would have my own career, my own money, and build a life that was my own. And I did that. However, in the process, I did not recognize that I was suppressing my entrepreneurial spirit. The safe corporate route was one I learned well, but in my heart, I was wanting more adventure and flexibility and the ability to choose my own schedule. I had always loved that but seemed to forget that was even an option as I became more entrenched in the corporate world. Had I not been willing to explore and experiment and try new things, I never would have known this about myself.

If I can give you any advice throughout this book, it is to give yourself lots of grace during this exploration. To allow yourself to explore and try new things and not to beat yourself up. This is one of the biggest challenges that most of us have.

We want to try something new and be perfect at it right away, even when we've never done it before.

That's simply not helpful and can keep us stuck in a cycle of shame and spinning in confusion. When I hosted my podcast, *Right Where You Are*, the one question I asked every guest was what they would say to someone who felt stuck. I now know that was the answer I was continually trying to answer for myself. I felt stuck and wanted to know how to keep moving forward and find myself in the process.

The journey to living unapologetically is filled with unknowns and questions and doubts. It's completely normal because most of us have forgotten who we are. That young child who knew exactly who they were and who did not apologize to anyone has somehow gotten buried in our subconscious and it takes some work to excavate. But that child is still in there and waiting for you to remember some of the amazing qualities and fun that makes you uniquely you.

One of the most helpful questions at the beginning of my journey was to ask myself what I wanted to be when I grew up.

What did I enjoy as a kid?

What was I obsessed with?

What did I love?

Asking myself these questions helped me to remember that I loved to write when I was younger. I wrote poems, soap operas, and tons of handwritten notes and letters to my friends. It helped me remember that I was a writer! I also loved to play school in my basement. I would line up the desks and chairs and stand at the front and teach my stuffed animals and Barbie dolls for hours on end. My mom always thought I would be a school teacher, but I had no desire to teach school. But isn't it fascinating that I am now a teacher through coaching and writing and sharing my ideas with others? I also always knew I had a calming presence. People felt seen and at peace with me. I created safe spaces for people to be themselves. I've always done this, I just wasn't always able to recognize it.

So let me ask you:

What did you love as a kid?

What made you light up and excited you?

What do you remember doing for hours on end without a care in the world?

Take some time and write about it. Don't judge it or ignore what comes up. You never know what pieces might come to your awareness after you allow yourself to remember. Be willing to experiment and have some fun with this!

Notes

CHAPTER FOUR

WHAT WORKS FOR YOU?

Many of us learn to listen to what everyone else says we should or shouldn't do in order to decide how we show up and what we do. This starts really early on in our lives, as teachers, coaches, and parents dictate what we do with our lives and how we do it.

There is value in this as we are growing, but it can also become a hindrance as we get older. Because then we are constantly looking for others to tell us what or who to be.

This tendency to put others' opinions and decisions ahead of our own happens when we don't pay attention to the rhythms of our bodies and our minds.

Because we have been told who we should be and what we should do, we learn to stop listening to our own inner intuition, because it typically doesn't align with what someone else is telling us. The reason is because they are not us! They are themselves. But somewhere in our culture, it's become completely normal to expect everyone to fall into line and to do things all the same. This is crazy when you think about it! We are all wired uniquely with different talents, desires, and ways of seeing the world. We have it when we are young. We are very connected to what we like and don't like and don't care if someone else doesn't understand it.

Think about this in terms of our bodies and our rhythms. As babies and young children, we naturally discovered what we preferred, and hopefully, our parents did too as they grew accustomed to what we liked and didn't like. We cried when we were hungry, we slept when we wanted to sleep. We listened to our bodies and rhythms, because we didn't have language to say differently and weren't accustomed to having to do it in a way someone else wanted us to. Even as children, we all had natural rhythms of waking up and what we preferred and didn't prefer when it came to foods and activities. As parents, this can be challenging because we want our kids to like the things that we like. But the reality is that sometimes they just don't. And it is totally okay.

As we get older, we start to separate and compartmentalize our thoughts and feelings and who we are.

We don't ask ourselves what we actually want, because we spend so much time trying to make other people happy or to fit into a box that someone else has created for us.

If this is resonating with you, you might be tempted to start to beat yourself up. I want to caution you not to go down that road. Just notice that you can relate to this and that it could be describing you. We will go into this in more detail a little later in the book.

This can be really unsettling at first because it goes against everything we've been told. We've been told we should just listen and follow instructions and do what is "right" and there is a proper way to do things. Again, I think this is important as we learn to grow and learn about life in general, but it often holds us back. And, our parents had their own conditioning they were dealing with as well that we often took on as our own.

As I mentioned, I made the decision that I was going to pursue a degree in business. It interested me and I knew there was a potential to make a very good living. I had big dreams and goals. I wanted to make a lot of money, and I intentionally wanted my own career that didn't depend on a man or someone else to tell me how much money I could make. That led me to a career in sales. I didn't want to lead people. I wanted to be on my own and make as much money as was available to me. And that worked for me for almost two decades. It was a great learning experience in how to cold call and prospect for customers and put myself out there in a way that was very uncomfortable at first. It really helped me grow as a person and get comfortable speaking and engaging with people in a variety of different industries.

I could have done this for a long time, but I started to pay attention to something that I hadn't really listened to for a long time: my intuition. Do you know that we all have internal guidance systems that are unique to us? We know this when we're younger, but then we often forget. We get caught up in the systems and processes that other people tell us we should do and forget that we are the ones who know ourselves the best. We start to believe that a parent, teacher, or someone else knows us better than we know ourselves. And that is simply not true. Our intuition is simply our ability to understand something instinctively, and it is what helps us know when we are on the right path and if what we are doing is in alignment with who we are at our core. It gets complicated, though, when we can do something and we can do it pretty well, so we start to confuse whether we really understand our intuition or not. Like being in a career that seems to make sense for us financially, but isn't fulfilling or bringing us life at all. Many of us spend our lives living this way. We simply tell ourselves we just have to suck it up until we retire and then we can do what we want.

That may work for you and you may be completely okay with that, but I wonder how many of us really ask ourselves if that's what we truly want. Do we really want to spend 20-40 years of our lives hating what we do simply so we can look forward to retiring someday and then start living?

For me, that question was answered very early on, as my dad passed away at age 53. He didn't subscribe to the "hate what you do until you retire" mentality, but he did have lots of things he wanted to do. Places he wanted to visit, experiences he wanted to have, and people he wanted to meet. He didn't get the opportunity to do many of those things, and he never had the opportunity to retire. It set me on a path to want to live life fully and experience as much as I could in the moment. Because retirement isn't guaranteed to any of us.

I also didn't love the idea of not liking my career for such a long time. Nothing about that felt right to me. I love the line in Shawshank Redemption that says, "Get busy living or get busy dying." I think that's so true. We always get the choice of whether we want to live or allow ourselves to slowly die. I know it sounds morbid to think about, but coming from someone who has experienced significant amounts of death in her life, it's a reality we will all face. Of course, we don't want it to be anytime soon, but none of us know that.

When I started to wake up to the idea that there could be something completely different and unique out there for me, I held on to this idea of figuring out what works for me. I've since learned that this is a part of my human design. I have a built-in desire to want to do things my own way and in alignment with who I am. But I didn't always know that consciously. I know now that my intuition has always been guiding me to do things that are outside of the norm and to look at situations differently than many people do.

And however your intuition is guiding you, I want to give you permission to explore what works for you.

To take some time and experiment and try some new things. Take a dance class, travel to a new place, take singing lessons, play in a band, start running, adopt an exotic pet, start a blog, paint, sculpt, restore a classic car. Do something new! I don't know what it is for you that will help you to see things differently and explore passions that may have been lying dormant, but I want to encourage you to think about what works for you.

It may mean that you start to research what other people are doing first. You read and listen and absorb the ideas of others like I did in the beginning. Or you may want to completely venture out on your own because you know exactly what it is that will light you up. The key is to make it your own. To allow yourself to dream and take a risk and try something new. In a way that feels authentic to you.

When you start trying new things and experimenting, it doesn't mean that people around you won't have their opinions. Trust me when I tell you that if you have been living a comfortable life without a lot of interruptions, if you start trying new things and experimenting with what makes you come alive, people will start to notice. And it's totally okay. The challenge is that many of the people that we think will support and encourage us are too close to us and may even freak out a little. Their love for us often comes out a little sideways, and their fear shows more than their love. Especially if we're in the midlife range. Ever hear of the midlife crisis? This is what most people will typically label your actions as when you're exploring. And because that wording has such a strong stigma, it may also make your friends and family nervous. What will she do? What's going on with her? What is happening? Even if you aren't in the midlife range, people typically tend to like the idea of change more than the actual change, which is why it can be so fearful for others to watch you trying new things.

When we start to change and try new things, it can bring up lots of insecurity in those around us.

It doesn't typically sound like it's their insecurity. It typically sounds like questions and judgment on you. So being aware that this will happen can be very helpful. It may also be a good idea to start to let your spouse or friends know what is going on with you. And to assure them that they don't need to worry as you embark on this journey of self-discovery. It can actually lead to feeling more alive and free, which can impact your relationships in really healthy ways, as long as you are willing to talk about it and be open about what you are experiencing.

It's also very helpful not to expect others to be where you are or to join you on the journey. I learned this lesson very early on, as with excitement and new discoveries, we want to share those with people who are close to us. I remember wanting my husband to be interested in the same things I was and to be where I was, but he just wasn't. While it frustrated me, I learned to recognize that he was supportive in his own way and his journey was not mine. We are all on our own journeys. The more you can remember that and not make it mean anything about you or about them, the more helpful it will be. You get to go on your own discovery journey, and when and if they're ready, they can go on their own.

As you explore, you may actually find that you love what you do. You've just been looking at it in a way that isn't helpful for you. We often tell ourselves stories that aren't helpful, but can't really see it until we take a step outside of it and ask ourselves some of these questions. Remember, this is your journey and you always get to decide what is helpful or not.

As you read this chapter, what is coming up for you?

What ideas are you thinking about that you'd like to try?

Don't judge what comes up as being too expensive, dangerous, or time consuming. Just let yourself dream a little bit about what might light you up.

Take some time and write about this in your journal.

Notes

CHAPTER FIVE

HONESTY

Learning to be totally honest with myself has been a continual journey for me. I'm still learning it. I always tell my clients that learning to look at ourselves objectively and make decisions from that place is continual work. It is how we continue to evolve and grow and become more fully ourselves. It isn't easy. And it takes work and determination, but it is so worth it.

It starts with getting really honest. And this is really hard for many of us. Because most of us have not had a safe space to do this. We've had our friends and family who know us well but who are also scared for us. Or maybe they've judged us for having the thoughts and feelings we've had. Judgment from others was something that I can see was a big part of my experience in the past.

It is really easy for people to judge when they don't understand or aren't willing to try to listen to a new perspective.

Or maybe someone made fun of your idea or you, and you've been fearful to express yourself honestly. There could be any number of things that have happened to us in the past and on this journey.

What so few of us have are people who can hold a safe space for us to be ourselves. Instead, we typically have people who are threatened or worried or commiserating with us and who find it easier to keep agreeing with us on a surface level. In order to do this work, it is helpful to have people who are willing to challenge us and see us for who we really are. When we have people like this who can help us see how we are thinking and feeling, it allows us to decide, on purpose, if we want to continue to behave that way. It helps us decide if our thoughts are helpful. This is what I found through coaching. Having a good coach who can help you see your thinking is a gift. We often want our friends to be able to help us do this, but sometimes it isn't possible. It's okay if you've never experienced this or had people to hold a safe space for you. Just know that it is available through a variety of possibilities.

And the good news is that we always get to decide how we show up. We get to decide what works for us and what doesn't. And that is the beauty of learning to be unapologetic. To actually ask ourselves what we want and then be willing to go after our desires. To state what we really want and to move towards living in alignment with those dreams. There is so much power when we take this approach. But taking these steps can also scare us. Fear can stop us from becoming unapologetic, because we're afraid of how others will think about us and what we are doing.

You've probably been told that other people have control over your feelings. That people have the power to hurt your feelings. But the reality is that simply isn't true. What you think about when someone says or does something is what causes you to feel a certain way. For example, if a stranger on the street tells you that you are an idiot, it probably doesn't mean much to you. You may shrug it off and forget about it quickly. But if someone you love calls you an idiot, you may have very different thoughts about it. You might wonder what you did to make them think that, or you may think that person is right and it makes you feel awful.

I know this can be so hard to understand at first, because this way of thinking typically wasn't modeled well for us. It's much easier to blame someone else for what we feel than to learn to understand that we have some power over our thoughts and feelings. You may not realize that you are doing this, and it is totally okay. I didn't realize I was doing this either until I started to understand the power of my own thoughts and feelings. Before I understood this, I would often try to get affirmation and validation from other people. I thought if I made enough money and was successful that I would feel good and others would recognize me and that would make me feel powerful. I thought if I helped enough people, they would see what a good person I was and tell me so I could feel good. I thought this would help me feel okay about myself. When in actuality, the only way I could learn to feel good about myself was through understanding the power of my own thoughts and feelings and deciding, on purpose, how I wanted to think and feel.

When I learned to understand this, it changed everything. It helped me see that life is mine for the making. My thoughts drive my feelings, and my feelings determine my actions. And when I truly grasped that and learned to decide, on purpose, how I want to feel, it was incredibly powerful! Because then nobody can ever take away my power. I am the only one who can give my personal power away and when I understand this, nobody can tell me how I should or shouldn't feel. Ever.

It definitely seems that this is not taught to us on purpose. Because if we truly understood this and knew it at our core, we would never allow ourselves to be controlled by outside forces or institutions. We would know that nobody can take our power away, and therefore, nobody can give it to us either. The power comes from how we think and feel and what we decide to do on purpose.

If thinking about this scares the shit out of you, you are not alone. It certainly did to me at first. I often wondered what it would feel like to not constantly be trying to prove myself or show others how valuable I am. I wondered how I could actually do this work on myself and what it would feel like to no longer blame someone else for anything. How would I ever learn to do that? And how could I move forward knowing this?

I truly believed that someone else had my answers and knew better than me. Maybe you have believed that, too. I have learned that is simply not true. The only person who knows exactly what you want and who you are is YOU! Period. Not even your parents or your siblings or your spouse. You are the only one who can decide what you want and WHY you want it! You are the only one who lives your life.

Maybe you have forgotten this. You've been so stuck in the routine that you've been living in and the life that you've created that you can't even imagine what it's like to know what you want and why you want it. And that's okay. I was there in the beginning, too. I couldn't imagine doing things simply because I wanted to or because they felt right to me, even when it went against what society or someone else thinks I should do. If this is you, too, know that you are not alone. And if you want to take steps towards learning to live authentically and stop apologizing for who you are and what you love, then make a decision right now to take a step forward on this journey.

Make a decision right now to get really honest with yourself about your life. About how you are living and whether it feels good or whether it is stifling you.

What are you actually feeling? Do you know? Can you name it? Or pinpoint where you feel it in your body?

We tend to think that we can't be really honest with ourselves because then we will beat ourselves up and spiral down a hole into depression. But the key is to knowingly go into this as an observer. As someone who is open to see themselves in a new way. As someone who is open from a standpoint of curiosity and awareness instead of judgment.

Here are a few questions to get started. Grab your journal or write in the margins.

Are you being honest with yourself about your life?

How would you describe your level of satisfaction with your life?

On a scale of 1-10, rate your level of happiness. Why did you rate it this number?

Do you feel fulfilled? Or empty? Or somewhere in between?

Are there any patterns you are continually seeing that sabotage your dreams?

Spend some time journaling about these questions and notice how you are feeling in your body. Does it feel tense and anxious? Or open? Remember to be curious as you notice these answers.

Learning to feel emotions in our bodies is a great way to take a step towards understanding ourselves.

Notes

CHAPTER SIX

PERMISSION

Our entire lives we are trained to ask for permission. From the time we are little, we are asking our parents for permission to do things. It becomes a way of life for us. We are told when we can do things and for how long and with whom. We are told to wait, to ask for permission to go to the bathroom, to get ready, and what we can and cannot do.

What happens over time is that our own knowing and belief in our own inner voice is completely silenced. We think someone else has our answers and that if we keep searching, we will find the answer. We will have the permission we need and everything will be perfect. It's simply not true. Nobody else has our answers and nobody needs to give us permission to do anything.

I hear what you're thinking in your head. "Yeah, but Tammy... what about our kids and teaching them to ask for permission?" I'm not talking to your kids. I'm talking to you. Giving our kids permission is a topic for a completely different book. I'm talking to the adult who has purchased this book with their own money and who has their own life. I'm talking to the grown adult who gets to decide what they do and do not like. The one who gets to say whether they will or won't do something, and when. We all have this power. We've just simply forgotten. Over and over again.

Because the reality is that it's easier to wait for permission. It keeps us "safe" in our minds. And it keeps us from taking our own responsibility for our lives. It keeps us stuck being average. It keeps us playing small. It keeps us living normal, ordinary lives.

And if that is what you want, own it. If you love your life and your decisions, own it and don't apologize for it. I'm not here to tell you that you need to do something with your life or you need to make a big drastic change. You absolutely don't have to. Because only you know what you want and what works for you.

But if you are reading this and something is stirring in your heart and soul for something different or bigger or unknown, then maybe it's time to start paying attention.

And maybe you do need permission for now. You need someone to tell you that it's perfectly okay to want the desires in your heart. It is okay to want more. It is okay to dream. I'm here to tell you it is!

When I knew I wanted something more, I looked for permission, too. I thought if I just went to enough conferences and made the right connections and found that one specific person with the secret answer, they would give me permission. When in reality, I was the only one whose permission I really needed. However, we typically don't know that right away. So I borrowed permission from someone I respected and looked up to. So if you also feel like you need it, I'm giving you permission. Right now. For whatever you think you need it for. For whatever you've been holding back, waiting to do. Borrow my belief and the permission to take the next step towards what you want.

The world was telling me that the life I had and the business I was in was enough. It was good and I was successful and I could keep climbing the corporate ladder and I would feel great. But I didn't. I could do it. I was good at it. But something was stirring in me and pulling me to look for more. To think outside the box and to open myself up to new possibilities that were outside of what normal had become for me. So rather than waiting for someone to give me permission, I just allowed myself to move forward. To keep experimenting and taking steps on this journey.

I had no idea where the journey would take me. And that scares so many of us, doesn't it? We want to know all the details. We want to know what is going to happen. We want someone to tell us exactly when and where it will all play out. But dreaming and living into who you were created to be doesn't work like that. It requires learning to listen to our soul and our intuition. It requires questioning our beliefs. It requires asking yourself if what you think is true really is. And that is hard work. It can take years. Or it can be quick. Every person's journey is different. For me, it meant leaning into creativity and learning to see myself in a different light. Remembering some of my gifts and allowing myself to learn to express them again. I had forgotten and had neglected them for quite a while.

Permission comes in lots of different forms. It can be in a dream, through the voice of a friend or mentor, or it can come from you. But if none of those have worked, let me give it to you now. You have permission to be you. You have permission to create a life you love. You have permission to dream and to explore and to be fully you.

So let me ask you:

Where are you waiting for permission?

What have you been telling yourself you can't possibly do?

What would you do if you felt like you had the permission you're seeking?

Notes

CHAPTER SEVEN

GET OUT OF YOUR OWN HEAD

Once you have permission, the next step is starting to learn to get past the thought process that what you do or say really matters all that much to anyone else. Seriously. We believe that people are always thinking about us. We obsess over what we think they are thinking about us. And most of the time, it's simply not true. People are stuck in their own heads and worrying about themselves and what others are thinking about them. This takes lots of practice, as we've been conditioned to think that what other people think about us is our business. It's not. Because as much as we try, we can never control what someone else is thinking. Ever. Oh, we think we can. We think if we just do the right things and act the right way that people will like us, and everything will be right in the world. But the reality is that what WE think of ourselves is what matters.

No, this is not from an egotistical standpoint that we are better than others or more enlightened, etc. It simply means that we start to know ourselves and our thoughts and then decide, on purpose, what we want to think about. This requires us to learn to look at ourselves objectively. To take a step back and start to see ourselves as objectively as we can. We've been taught that we ARE our thoughts and feelings. But that's not true. We're experiencing thoughts and feelings, which are part of the human experience. We are all given these thoughts and emotions as part of the deal of being here on earth. But what happens as we get older is that we start to judge ourselves and beat ourselves up for simply being ourselves. And then we just stay stuck in a spin cycle of thoughts and feelings that feel completely out of control. It's what drives many of us to look for ways to buffer through alcohol, drugs, sex, working out, or _____.

Learning to understand yourself starts with getting out of your own head.

If you go through life worrying about what people think more than you care about what YOU think, that's what keeps us stuck.

The people you truly care about know who you are and get you. But also, it's time for YOU to get to know and understand yourself.

Because at some point in your life, you get tired of trying to please everyone. I know this seems hard to comprehend. Especially for those of us that have been trained to put others before ourselves. It's how many of us received love and affirmation and validation throughout most of our lives. I rocked the people-pleasing game (or so I thought) for a good chunk of my life. I knew exactly how to play the roles that were acceptable and "good" and would help me earn praise and affirmation from teachers, coaches, adults, and friends. I was a master at being in the middle of everything so that I could help coordinate and communicate and be needed. If I wasn't taking on something that wasn't my own to take on, I didn't know who I was.

The challenge was, I never learned how to pay attention to myself. To do the things that I wanted to do in life. To actually have an opinion and desires for myself and not just for other people. Again, this is so conditioned in our culture that many of us never question it. We do what we've been told. We put others first and don't think about ourselves or our own wants and desires. Because that would mean we're not following the rules or being "good." We are conditioned through education, religion, business, and family dynamics. We learn how to play the game and can end up spending most of our life chasing some impossible goal to make others happy, and hopefully, in turn, they will validate us so we feel worthy. We simply aren't taught this for a variety of reasons. And many of us can get caught up in trying to find those reasons and fix them instead of simply understanding it and knowing that we have the power to choose differently.

This is something that has dramatically changed my life. The ability to decide, on purpose, for myself. We can do it every day. We get to choose our thoughts and feelings and how we respond to everything. We don't always understand this, again, because we've been told that life just happens to us and then we either react or respond. But the reality is that we can learn how to understand our thoughts and feelings and intentionally decide how we want to think and feel. This was a huge light bulb moment for me. I didn't have to respond or react in a certain way just because that is what I was used to doing. I could decide, on purpose, how I wanted to respond.

Even before I really understood this, I was doing this in my own way with my kids. When you become a parent, there are all kinds of expectations and traditions and ways of doing things that we learn. We learn this from how we were brought up and what we were taught. I was a really picky eater as a kid and absolutely hated that my parents made me try all kinds of things that I didn't like and didn't want. My dad was a hunter and always was trying to pass off animals that he hunted that grossed me out. I was on to him, though! So when I became a parent and my first son was an extremely picky eater, I naturally chose the ways that I had been taught. You eat what's on your plate, you don't complain about it, and you battle every mealtime. I tried that for a little while and then decided it didn't work for us. There were plenty of battles that I was facing with this child, and I decided early on that dinner time was not going to be one of them.

Now, people have their opinions about this, for sure. People certainly told me what they thought about my decision not to make my child eat things he hated. But it was my decision and I owned it. I did not let people's thoughts and comments and opinions about the way I was parenting him mean anything to me. It was simply their opinion. Period. They were free to express it, but I didn't have to take it on. There are so many examples of this in all of our lives. We do things because that's how our parents did it or ingrained in our heads that it was the only way to do something. What if that simply isn't true?

One of the biggest lessons I've learned is that life is not black and white. Decisions aren't always right or wrong. This is called dualistic thinking and Father Richard Rohr taught me so much about this.

> *"Dualistic thinking is our way of reading reality from the position of our private and small self. 'What's in it for me?' 'How will I look if I do this?' This is the ego's preferred way of seeing reality. It is the ordinary 'hardware' of almost all Western people. The dualistic mind is essentially binary, either/or thinking. It knows by comparison, opposition, and differentiation. It uses descriptive words like good/evil, pretty/ugly, smart/stupid, not realizing there may be a hundred degrees between the two ends of each spectrum." Father Richard Rohr*

Are there always only one or two ways to do something? Much of the world would say there is, but it simply isn't true. Our experiences, our lives, and our upbringings are all different. And what works for one of us simply doesn't work for someone else. We can judge it and get upset about it and try to make people see it our way, or we can learn to understand and OWN our decisions. We can learn to live in alignment with who we are and not apologize for it. Because when you understand this, you stop trying to change other people and the way they act and what they say. Because when we live in alignment with who we are, we give permission and space for others to do the same. It is incredibly freeing and a gift, not only to ourselves but to the people and the world around us.

This requires us to learn to ask WHY and to question things that don't seem to work for us. Some call it critical thinking, or learning to ask questions and not just automatically accepting what someone else tells us. Again, this isn't a tool that we are often taught in school, because much of the way our education system is designed is to teach you something in a very specific way. It's kind of crazy when you think about it, because our education system was developed in the age of the industrial revolution. It has needed some serious updates over the years, as most of the world is no longer being trained to be factory workers, but that is what the original intent was. This was so eye-opening to me. If you're interested in seeing the education system from a different perspective, check out Sir Ken Robinson's TED Talk on Youtube. It will help you see why the education system is not designed for multiple types of learning or unique ways that many kids learn best.

I have learned this first hand through our own parenting experience. I could never understand why I was so different from my brother and sister when we grew up in the same house with the same parents. But we are all very different. The moment I had my second child, I understood it completely. We are wired uniquely from the minute we make our appearance on this earth. We have different ways of seeing the world and experiencing it. We have different likes and dislikes and ways of how we want to be comforted.

My oldest son had incredible challenges sleeping as a baby. The main place he wanted to sleep was in my arms. Anything else was not okay for him. I remember being very distraught trying to figure this out as a new mom who was sleep-deprived. It took some trial and error and we figured out what worked for him. It was nothing that they told me in the *What to Expect When You're Expecting* book. That is for sure! And then when my second son came along, he could sleep anywhere and whenever. It was so crazy to me! Learning to understand their likes and dislikes was the precursor to me starting to ask myself my own questions. It would take quite a few years. Those young child years can be pretty overwhelming and full of constant questioning about our decisions. That didn't always leave much time to think about what I wanted.

I think this is what happens for most of us. We get caught up in our lives. Whether it's being a mom or dad, committed to our careers, or constantly trying to find the one thing that we think we are searching for. And in the process, we forget to ask ourselves what we really like and don't like. We are so used to being conditioned to put everyone and everything else in front of ourselves that we completely forget how to do this! I know when I first started asking myself what I really liked and what I wanted, I had absolutely no idea. It was almost as if I had lost a big piece of who I was in the process of taking care of everyone else. We don't realize this consciously much of the time, as the responsibility and challenge of adulthood sometimes just takes over.

It's easy to start to realize this and then immediately go to beating ourselves up for it and wonder how in the world this could have happened. But I want to caution you to try not to do that. First of all, because the past is the past and there is nothing you can do to go back and change it. Oh, we think if we stress and obsess about it, it will change. But that's simply not true.

———

What if, instead of beating ourselves up, we learned how to be very curious and to ask ourselves questions? What if we took time to get to know ourselves in a new way, almost like we would do if we were meeting a new friend and learning all about them? What might happen then?

Here are a few questions that might help you as you begin this process.

What sets you apart from your siblings and family that might speak to your uniqueness?

Are there aspects of your past that seem to have made an impact on your expectations of yourself?

What part of your life has overshadowed your journey to YOU?

If you were getting to know yourself for the first time, what would you hope to hear or learn?

Notes

CHAPTER EIGHT

GET CURIOUS

After you have asked yourself these questions, you may start to get a little frustrated. Let me tell you that it is totally okay. It's natural to ask ourselves how we got here, how we could possibly forget what we loved, and how life turned out the way it did. This might be because you remember a dream or remember that you just simply stopped doing something you absolutely love. And that might make you mad. You may instantly want to blame someone. Your parents, your spouse, your kids. I want to caution you to recognize this and interrupt it.

Is it easier to blame someone else for something? Absolutely! Because it takes all the responsibility off of you. And we don't typically like to be responsible for our own behavior. It's much easier to say it is because of what someone else did or didn't do. But all of the concepts we're talking about so far require us to take responsibility for who we are and how we show up in the world. So, be curious and ask yourself questions and start to think about your life in a very curious way. But also be willing to take responsibility for your own actions. This is a huge step in emotional health. At the end of the day, we make our own decisions, regardless of whatever circumstances we have encountered. We choose how and if we show up, as well as how we respond to whatever is happening.

This is why I advise all of my clients to be really curious about their thoughts and feelings and what they are remembering. Because curiosity has a very different energy than judgment or condemnation. It is full of hope and possibility and an opportunity to learn about ourselves. That's what we're working towards. Learning about ourselves in a way that is new and fresh, but also feels very aligned with who we are. Many of us have lived out of alignment with who we are for a long time. So, of course, it is going to take some time for us to remember who we are. I want to caution you to be gentle and loving with yourself in this process. Any time your brain wants to go to judgment and beating yourself up, interrupt it by asking this question, "How can I be more curious about myself today?"

The definition of curious is to be eager to know or learn something. We are so used to being curious about other people and situations, but we aren't usually accustomed to being curious about ourselves. Because we think we know ourselves already and there is nothing to learn. But what if that isn't true?

What if you are telling yourself a story about who you are but have forgotten some of the most amazing things about yourself?

Or, what if you are telling yourself a story that wasn't yours to begin with? What would that mean?

I often coach clients to realize that the story they've been telling themselves about who they are and what they can do in the world is simply a limiting belief. And sometimes it isn't even their belief! Sometimes it is from a parent, someone from their life growing up, or a norm society has given us that we don't even believe!

Being curious starts with paying attention to our thoughts and stories and then looking at them objectively without judgment. We haven't been taught this. We've been taught to beat ourselves up and to make fun of ourselves for even considering such a thing! One of the things I often say to myself when recognizing thoughts that don't serve me is, "Isn't this interesting?" Or, "Isn't it interesting that my brain immediately went to that thought?" This helps us look at it from an objective standpoint instead of instantly going into fix-it mode. That's the other challenge we often have. When we recognize something, we immediately want to make it go away or fix it, as if something is wrong with us. Again, we've been conditioned to do this, so don't be so hard on yourself when you realize this.

So, how can you be more curious about YOU today?

What would it look like to look at yourself with curiosity and without judgment?

Notes

CHAPTER NINE

SELFISH

One of the reasons many of us have not done the work to figure out who we are and to spend time on ourselves is because we have bought the lie that it is selfish to do so. Many of us were taught to believe that we should be the absolute last person on the list. Always. It is a badge of honor and something that many people teach as a way of selfless service to others. Don't get me wrong. I am NOT against serving others. In fact, I identify as an Enneagram 2, and this is a part of who I am. If you're not familiar with the Enneagram, it is an ancient personality typing system that helps you understand how you view the world. I highly recommend checking out Ian Morgan Cron's book, *The Road Back to You*, if you are interested in learning more.

One of the things I know about myself is that I love to help and support others. But, the catch is, when I do this and don't take care of myself, I often get resentful and upset because everyone else's needs come before my own. If this is a tendency for you also, it may be because you have not ever considered what your own needs are.

I operated with these tendencies for most of my life. I was trained that it is good and honorable to take care of everyone else. To think of others more than myself, to always put their thoughts and needs before my own, and to never ask for anything in return. This can be a harmful way to live, friends. Because as the old saying goes, "You can't pour from an empty cup." When we are constantly living for and serving others despite our own needs, we typically don't take care of ourselves. We don't do things that rejuvenate our souls and fill our own cups in the process. We can tend to burn out in service to others and feel resentful. We see this in nonprofits and churches and humanitarian causes all the time. We think we are helping and doing an amazing job to serve others, but we haven't taken the necessary steps to take care of ourselves first. It doesn't mean that you don't help. It simply means that you learn to help from a healthier place instead of from a depleted posture.

A healthier posture looks different for everyone. For me, it meant that I never even asked myself what I wanted. I got validation and praise and affirmation from other people for helping, so I never took the time to ask myself what I wanted. My needs were last, and I was too exhausted to do anything about them after serving others for so long. This is not a sustainable model, no matter what anyone tells you. Because your health, your mindset, and your spirituality are important parts of keeping yourself in alignment and living authentically. When we are constantly giving to others and never allowing ourselves to receive, we will eventually burn out or quit.

Self-care has become a big topic over the last few years as more and more people realize that they can only work so hard and neglect their own spiritual, mental, and physical health for so long.

We can only be disconnected from ourselves for an amount of time before crashing and burning out.

Many people confuse self-care with being selfish. But there is a big difference. Self-care is taking care of you so that you can show up in the world in a healthy way. Being selfish is doing things only for yourself and wanting to cause harm to others in the process. That's a big difference!

And here's the thing: my self-care looks different than yours. I have experimented and learned what works for me, and it is always different than what works for my husband, clients, or friends. I have learned that being in nature is essential to me, as is moving my body and prioritizing sleep. I spend time in meditation and journaling and intentionally unplugging from social media and devices. But for you, it might be something completely different. It might be listening to great music, playing a musical instrument, reading, working out, getting a massage, sitting in silence, or being with family. Only you know what helps you to be calm and relax and decompress from life. If you have not been intentionally doing these things, it will feel awkward and unsettling at first. And that is totally okay. I remember starting to do things for myself and feeling incredibly guilty and unproductive. Because many of us have bought the lie that we are supposed to be constant producers in order to earn our worth and be a good human. I call bullshit on that idea. I did that for many years of my life and was on the verge of adrenal failure because of it. As I mentioned, nature has been a huge component of my journey. Learning to get outside, to soak in the beauty, and grounding myself by being in the forest or simply walking outside has been so helpful for me. Learning to take care of yourself and intentionally deciding how you choose to think about it is the key.

***

Ask yourself right now:

When was the last time you intentionally took time to care for yourself?

When did you do something that brings you joy or helped create a sense of calm in your life?

What did you do?

How did you feel while you were doing it?

We'll talk more about this in the coming chapters, but here are a few questions to consider.

Do you have thoughts that self-care is selfish? Why?

Is it possible to look at it differently?

Think about what you like to do that calms you. Make a list.

If you could do one thing today to take care of you, what would it be?

Notes

CHAPTER TEN

MINDSET

We tell ourselves stories all the time. Stories that we think are truths. Stories that are not helpful for us. We can call these thoughts or stories or tapes playing in our minds. And after many years, these thoughts and stories seem like they are truths. And we don't question them. We simply agree with the stories and let them build over time. Have you ever played the game telephone? Where one person starts with a story and then whispers it to the next person, who repeats what they heard, and you keep going around the circle. The last person says what was originally said. Have you ever played a game where it was exactly the same? I certainly haven't. The same thing happens to the stories in our brains. They start to take on a life of their own and we add our own drama and interpretation to them and they become much bigger than the original. We do this in our own brains all the time. And it becomes a spin cycle that eventually feels like truth to us.

Beliefs are simply thoughts that we have learned to repeat over time.

Dr. Nicole LePera, known as The Holistic Psychologist, says in her book, *How to Do the Work*, "A belief is a practiced thought grounded in lived experience. Beliefs are built up over years of thought patterns and require both interior and exterior validation to thrive." It's not just a thought because most of us have evidence to show us that it really could be true. But the key is that we don't often question it. We've taken on other people's beliefs as our own in so many different areas of our lives that we don't even realize it. I did this for most of my life. I took the beliefs of people around me and bought into them as my own. I wasn't really taught to question ideas or other people's thoughts. And looking back, I also think the reason I didn't question many of these things is because I hadn't decided for myself what I thought and believed. I learned from others and trusted their advice. I think this happens to most of us as we are growing up because that is part of the process.

It wasn't until my 30's that I really started to wonder what life would look like if I actually decided for myself what I believed and formed my own opinions about a variety of things.

So many of us don't do this because we are afraid of what we will discover. Or if we pull on one string of thought then it will unravel everything that we've ever believed and trusted to be true. And I understand how that can be overwhelming and seem challenging. That's why this work takes time, patience, and a willingness to trust ourselves in the process.

As a life and business mindset coach, I work with many of my clients on learning to understand their minds and the thoughts that they are continually having. We have so many thoughts that we don't even notice many of them. It's been said that we have something like 60,000 thoughts per day, so it's no wonder that our brain picks and chooses which ones to listen to. But what we often don't realize is that our thoughts and mindset can be the exact thing that is holding us back from a life we really want. It can be holding us back from that promotion, partner, business, or life decision that we really want. Understanding this even on a basic level can change everything. If we truly do have the ability to deliberately think thoughts, on purpose, that are helpful, what could that change in our lives?

This was so new for me. While I believed in, and practiced, positive affirmations and tried to have a positive attitude, I still often felt like life was happening to me all the time. Like I didn't have control over the circumstances that life would present to me. The new job, the partner, the place I chose to live. I guess I thought most of that was due to my decision but also had a lot to do with luck and chance. And it does to some degree. However, the deeper I have gone into this work, the more I have come to understand that we always get to choose our thoughts. And those thoughts create our feelings. We've been taught that our thoughts and feelings just happen to us. And life just happens to us. But what if that isn't true? What if we have more power over our thoughts and feelings than we've ever known?

This idea is not new. It's been around since the beginning of time. People have talked about it in different ways and still do, but the idea is the same. Our thoughts practiced over time become our beliefs. Those thoughts and beliefs create feelings in our body, which then lead us to actions (or inaction) and drive a result. I had heard this before, but discovering Brooke Castillo from The Life Coach School really solidified this idea for me. She hosts a podcast and trains coaches in the life coach industry. She has simplified this concept into what she calls The Model. When I heard her explain this, it made complete sense. You can use her model to objectively see your thoughts and feelings and determine how it is driving your actions and your results. She has created a business using and teaching this model that has created millions of dollars in revenue and has trans-formed the life coaching industry with her work.

Being able to look at your thoughts objectively takes practice, mainly because we have been taught over the years that we ARE our thoughts and feelings. They determine who we are. Rather than understanding we are humans experiencing thoughts and feelings that are perfectly normal. Do you see the difference? Read that again if you need to. You are not your thoughts. You are not your feelings. You are simply a human being experiencing those things that are perfectly natural. How does that feel to read that? For me, it was so freeing.

I remember coaching someone early on through a situation where she was describing how she was feeling about a friend. I said, "It sounds like you are feeling jealous." Her quick response was an emphatic, "Absolutely not! I am NOT a jealous person!" I had to remind her that I had not said she was a jealous person. I had pointed out that she was EXPERIENCING jealousy. Do you see the difference? Understanding this alone can transform your life. Seriously. I know you might be thinking that this is too simple to possibly work, but I promise you that it does.

Learning to see our thoughts and feelings objectively is the key to creating a life that we want.

Awareness is always the first step, but then the ability to see how we are continually thinking and acting is the key that unlocks those hidden ways of self-sabotage and how we hold ourselves back. Think about something that you have wanted for a long time.

How do you talk about it?

Do you talk about it in an objective way that highlights how it is absolutely possible and you are open to it?

Or do you talk about it in a way that tells your mind you will never have it?

We don't think this makes a difference but it absolutely does! Let's look at an example.

Let's say that you started a business and you have an income goal of $100K. But you have never made more than $50K in the jobs you've held previously. What are you possibly thinking about that goal? You could be thinking that it is an impossible goal. You could be thinking that it will require you to work super hard in order to achieve it. You may be thinking that nobody in your family has ever had their own business that made that much money. You may think that it's going to require you to sacrifice everything you love in order to make it happen. And when you are thinking thoughts like this, most likely you are feeling frustrated or defeated because you really WANT to believe you can, but those thoughts just keep showing up.

Now think about what kinds of actions you take while thinking these thoughts and feeling frustrated or defeated. Do you keep going? Do you keep moving towards your goal? Do you try new ways of reaching customers? Do you experiment? Or do you get stuck in inaction? Typically, that's where most of my clients find themselves. Stuck in inaction. They know what they WANT to do, but they simply aren't doing it and they don't know why. That's when we dive into their thoughts.

What are you really thinking about the goal?

Are you thinking about the things I listed above? If so, then of course you are not moving towards your goal! It makes sense when you can objectively look at it this way.

Let's take another example. Let's say you want to lose 20 pounds. You may have thoughts like:

I've tried every diet imaginable.

I can't keep the weight off.

I will have to restrict my food and I don't like that.

I may be able to lose the weight, but I don't know how I can maintain a strict diet.

And when you think these unhelpful thoughts, you will most likely feel resistant or apathetic. You may feel overwhelmed and just say forget it all. Can anyone relate? I know many of us have been there and continue to work on this with ourselves. We want to change and we intellectually know all the steps to take, but we just don't do it. So much of this can be explained by the stories and the thoughts that we are continually thinking but often are not even aware of.

I've been working on my health journey for quite a few years and have had many of those thoughts I listed above. And a few years ago, I heard myself telling multiple people, "This is just what I do. I lose the weight and gain it back. It's my pattern." And after I heard myself say that a few times, I started to question why. Why do I keep repeating these patterns, even when I know I no longer want the same result? Utilizing these thought tools and looking at it objectively, I uncovered the belief I couldn't see that was underneath it all. I didn't think weight loss was sustainable for me. Mainly because I was losing it in ways that I was not committed to continuing on for the rest of my life. So of course it wouldn't be sustainable!

That was such a revelation for me and a key to understanding why I was continually stuck in the same pattern of losing and regaining weight. If everything in me didn't believe it was sustainable, of course, I was going to gain it all back! Sooner or later I would get frustrated with what I was doing and say, "Forget it! It's not worth it." This is still a journey I'm on, but learning to watch for, and question, the thoughts that are coming up has been so helpful for me.

So what about you?

What are some patterns that you are continually seeing in your life that you want to change?

Maybe it's in your business or career. You keep taking roles that you don't really want and that do not pay you what you are worth.

Or maybe it's in your relationships. You continue to sabotage the relationships because you don't know what you really want.

Or maybe it's in your own health journey. You know you feel better when you take care of yourself, but you never make the time to do it. I don't know what it is for you, but I want to encourage you to start looking at your thoughts and feelings objectively and ask yourself honestly if they are helpful for you.

––––––––

Here are a few questions that may be helpful in this process. And remember, this takes practice. Don't be so hard on yourself as you are learning this.

Think about a goal you have. Then recognize a thought.

Is this thought I'm thinking helpful in moving me towards my goal?

Is this something I would say to my child or someone else I loved?

Is it possible this thought is simply not true?

Start to explore your brain in a nonjudgmental and curious way, and see what comes up for you.

Notes

CHAPTER ELEVEN

FEEL YOUR FEELINGS

We've talked about our mindset and the stories we tell ourselves. I've also talked a little about feeling your feelings. And you may be wondering what that means. Because the reality is that most of us have never been taught to feel our feelings when they come up. We've been taught to suppress them or avoid them or hide them. Somehow, having feelings has been seen as a negative quality in our culture. And that is simply not true.

Feelings are simply a vibration in our body. We are all human and have been given a spectrum of feelings for a reason. The challenge is that many of us were taught that we should not feel our feelings. Because then we would BE our feelings. Feeling jealous would mean we were a jealous person, and that is not nice. Feeling anger meant that something was wrong with us, and we wanted to hurt others. Feeling empathy and compassion meant that we were soft-hearted and not tough. Feeling sadness meant that we would sink into a deep pit of despair.

Think back to your childhood. How were feelings discussed (or not discussed) in your families and communities? Were you allowed to feel your feelings without criticism or judgment? Sadly, msny of us weren't. The generations before us weren't always great at learning to manage emotions and feelings. They simply did not have the tools or understanding that we do now. I work with many clients to help them understand how their upbringing could be impacting their ability, or inability, to actually experience and feel their feelings. This is not from a place of blaming our parents or caregivers and saying we are the way we are because it's their fault. It's simply learning to recognize what was modeled about how to handle or avoid our feelings from those we lived with. And it may or may not have aligned with how you were needing or wanting to feel your feelings.

In her book, *How To Do The Work*, Dr. Nicole Lepera explains this in a very helpful way. She says, "Anyone with their own level of unresolved feelings will generally feel uncomfortable with a child's expression of feelings and may cope by trying to dismiss them. Children have legitimate feelings and look to be comforted and supported. But they are often told their pain is inconsequential."

If that hit you right in your heart, you are not alone. I have talked to so many friends and clients whose parents were not equipped to handle the strong feelings that they experienced as children.

And when we don't know how to handle something, we often try to control it or simply avoid it.

In my own experience, this looked like people shutting down and not talking or acknowledging feelings, or simply acting as if nothing was wrong at all. That can be really confusing as a child, because we are often so in touch with our feelings but don't know what to do with them.

This often leads to learning to suppress our emotions, numb them with alcohol, drugs, food, or simply refuse to allow ourselves to feel them. These approaches typically are not helpful. Our bodies need to be regulated, and these vibrations need to have somewhere to go. It is said that vibrations will pass through typically in about 90 seconds if we allow them and don't resist the emotions. But we don't understand that, so we put up resistance. And then the vibrations get stuck in our bodies. Did you know that trauma and unresolved feelings stay trapped in our bodies? That was a new concept for me when I first heard it, but it made total sense. You can learn more about it in the book *The Body Keeps the Score: Brain, Mind and Body in the Healing of Trauma* by Bessel van der Kolk M.D.

As you learn to be more unapologetic about who you are, it's helpful to understand your feelings and allow yourself to feel them. Because the things you feel can be incredibly helpful in rediscovering who you are. Since learning to feel my feelings and lean into what my body is trying to tell me, I have learned that I am extremely empathic. I feel other people's feelings and energy. I didn't understand this when I was younger. I would feel things deeply, but not understand why. I somehow thought this was a bad quality to have as I simply didn't understand it. But I've come to realize that it is a very special gift. It helps me be compassionate and allow people to be who they fully are in my presence without judgment. The more I learn to feel my feelings, the more understanding I am when others have their own unique, big feelings.

I understood this very clearly as I watched my son wrestle with very big feelings for a small little boy. He is even more empathic and feels the energy of others much deeper than I do. And he had no idea what to do with it. He is caring and loving. He is always looking out for other people and their feelings, but it often led to him defending others and then getting in trouble because of it. This has been such a big learning experience for all of us. My dad was a great model of not being afraid to show his feelings and not have any shame around it. I have always wanted my boys to have that same ability. A big part of learning to feel my feelings has also helped my boys as they learn to navigate their own feelings.

As you know, people have their own ideas and notions about feelings. Some feelings are acceptable. Some feelings are not, in their eyes. But the reality is that we are all human and have all of these feelings available to us. We are meant to experience our feelings. Every single one of them.

For example, I typically didn't allow myself to feel sadness and disappointment. It seemed like I experienced them so often that I finally refused to let myself feel them at all. Perhaps I thought I would go into some kind of downward spiral and never be able to get out of it. I have learned that simply is not true. When we allow ourselves to feel the vibrations of our feelings, they typically pass through much quicker and easier.

In her book, *The Gifts of Imperfection,* author Brene Brown says, "We cannot selectively numb emotions. When we numb the painful emotions, we also numb the positive emotions." That really resonated with me, as I had gotten to a place of being very even-tempered, and it took quite a bit to sway me one way or the other in regards to feelings. Since I had learned to not allow myself to feel sadness, I also wasn't allowing myself to feel joy. And that stinks! I've been learning to allow myself to feel whatever feelings come up and while, at first, it is unsettling, it is actually pretty amazing to learn to let yourself feel.

Are there specific feelings you don't allow yourself to feel? Maybe it's:

- *Sadness*
- *Frustration*
- *Anger*
- *Resentment*
- *Jealousy*
- *Hurt*

Ask yourself honestly.

It may be helpful to think of a big event in your life where you suppressed an emotion.

How did you feel?

Did you allow yourself to feel the feeling that matched the moment? Or did you keep it all inside?

Write a few thoughts about why you don't allow yourself to feel it or why you think you shouldn't.

Now ask yourself:

How do I want to feel?

This can be an eye-opening exercise for you. Be sure to give yourself grace in the process. It's so important!

Notes

CHAPTER TWELVE

EXPERIMENT

Now comes the fun part! We get to experiment. Somehow, we've lost the art of experimentation in our culture. We want everything to be planned out and every risk considered before taking action. What if that is not how we actually learn? What if we actually learn by experimenting and trying things and seeing if we like them? What a novel concept, right? This is what we do as kids when we try different subjects and sports and activities. We have to try them in order to find out if we like them. Just like those stinky vegetables our moms made us try.

This shift in thought from "I have to have everything figured out before I start" to "What if I could experiment" can change everything for you.

Instead of beating yourself up for not being good at something the first time you try it (which many of us do), you can actually have fun in the process. I remember wanting to try rollerblading after we got married. I saw so many people doing it, and it seemed like such a great workout. I had roller-skated like a boss in elementary and junior high, so I was confident I could pick it up easily. So I bought myself a pair of rollerblades and set out to try them out. I was an athlete and I figured, "How hard could it be?" Famous last words, right? I fell so many times the first time I put those roller blades on that I was sure I would break something. Thankfully, I didn't. But I also realized something else. I didn't really like it. I didn't like being higher up on the ground and not being able to stop. I did keep trying and could go farther distances after a few times, but in the end, it wasn't my thing. And I was totally okay with that.

Sometimes, as we get older, we stop trying new things because we believe this lie that we should already know how to do it and that we should have it perfected the very first time. How crazy is that? Did we expect our kids to know how to walk the first time they took a step? No! We knew they'd have to keep trying and keep falling down before they would eventually figure it out. What if we could look at remembering who we are and what we love to do as a similar experiment?

Think about something you've always wanted to try. What are the thoughts that come up about it? Do you think "Oh, I could never do that!" or "It sure would be nice to do that someday" or "That will never happen?"

Ask yourself why you instantly have negative thoughts about it. Are these thoughts helpful?

So much of the mindset work and noticing our thoughts and continual patterns is recognizing how we speak to ourselves and what that leads to. If we are constantly thinking that we could never do something, we will eventually talk ourselves out of it, won't we?

A few years ago, my family and I went to Sedona, AZ. Oh my goodness. What an amazing place it is. If you have never been, I highly recommend it to everyone. It is a natural healing place with breathtaking views. My boys were young and fearless at the time we went. So hiking and rock climbing to them was a no-brainer. Of course, we would climb up these really steep rocks and see what is up there. Why wouldn't we? And while I loved the idea of it, I was fearful at first. I had never rock climbed before. Sure, I'd hiked in the midwest through forests and paths, but we don't have mountains here. And while I wouldn't say I am afraid of heights, I do have a fear of falling and don't like looking down from high places.

We started off with a less intense hike on Bell Rock. It's pretty circular with not much height and climbing needed to get to a beautiful view. But at one point, as my boys had quickly climbed up above me, I found myself on the side of a rock where I needed to pull myself up in order to get to the next clearing or decide to jump back down. I was suspended on the side of a big boulder. And I completely froze and was unable to move. I started having a panic attack, as I couldn't imagine lifting my hand up to go up to the next part, and I also didn't want to jump back down. How long could I stay suspended on the side of this rock? With each breath, I started to feel more anxious and fearful. I was literally stuck and starting to freak out. I had convinced myself that I could climb these rocks, but could I really? Could I be willing to risk falling while I pulled myself up? I had no idea. I allowed myself to stay there for what seemed like an eternity, but in reality, was probably only a few minutes. My boys were looking down and encouraging me to come up because the view was amazing, and they were cheering me on that I could do it.

After a few deep breaths, I had to make a decision. I was either going to join them and see the amazing view, or I was going to allow myself to jump down.

I chose to move forward. I had some assistance, as they helped take my hand and guide me up, but I did it! I pushed through the emotions and the fear and was so glad I did, as the view was breathtaking. It also helped me to know that I can do something I set my mind to. I can still feel fear and uncertainty, but keep going. Had I not done that, I would never have been able to make the hike up Cathedral Rock the following day, which was much steeper and scarier. The view was worth every step to get there.

I would never have known I loved rock climbing and hiking in this way if I hadn't been open to the experience. Over the years, I have opened myself up to new experiments. A few included running my first 5K ever and going on to run three more 5Ks that summer. I also tried hot yoga, learning a new way to play the piano, podcasting, and so much more in between.

Take a minute and ask yourself what you have always wanted to try.

Let yourself dream. Don't exclude something just because you can't see how you could possibly do it right now. Make this a super fun dream list. It doesn't have to be big things like rock climbing or traveling. It can be all different kinds of things. Here are some options to consider:

- *Journaling*
- *Meditation*
- *Hiking*
- *Getting out in nature*
- *Watching the sunset*
- *Starting a new exercise routine*
- *Trying a new gym*
- *Taking a break from social media*
- *Intentionally unplugging one day a week*
- *Dancing*
- *Joining a choir*
- *Learning to play an instrument*
- *Traveling to a foreign country*
- *Learning a new language*
- *Inviting a neighbor over that you don't know*
- *Trying a new, local coffee shop*
- *Writing a blog*
- *Starting a podcast*
- *Getting up earlier to spend time alone*

What do YOU want to do? Write down your thoughts in your journal or inside this book.

Open yourself up to new possibilities. A great way to do this is to just start paying attention to yourself and your reactions when you see things.

Do you light up when you read a great book?

Do you come alive when your favorite song comes on?

Do you feel yourself calming down when you are in certain places?

Do you look forward to seeing certain people or participating in certain activities?

Remember that this is an experiment. You get to decide what you try, how often, and what resonates with you. Learning to notice this can be so helpful in finding things that you love and that bring you life. You may even surprise yourself with what you love. I resisted hot yoga because the first time I tried it I thought I was going to die. Literally. But I tried it again at a different studio and ended up loving it. The detoxification process and the reward at the end with a super cold washcloth always feels awesome to me.

Just a word of caution here. If you have been doing things the same way for quite a while and not really trying new things, this may come as a surprise to those around you.

People tend to want us to stay the same always and may question as you start to experiment. It's totally okay! Learning to find out what you like isn't about anyone else. It's about you. And while it may take some adjustments with scheduling and changing how you've always done things, this is a good thing. Trust that you will be okay no matter what comes up and that you can still take care of every-thing in your life that you normally do while also learning to try out some new things and experiment.

Take a few minutes and write out some things that you want to try. Remember, they can be simple and something that only matters to you. Don't judge your list or what you put on it. Start to catch yourself when you think "Wouldn't that be fun" or "I'd love to do that!" There is power in writing it down because sometimes we will surprise ourselves with what comes out of our subconscious that we have been wanting to try.

Have fun and experiment!

Notes

CHAPTER THIRTEEN

ACCEPTANCE

As we start to experiment, we will start to see things in ourselves that we haven't seen for a while, or even don't remember seeing. This is completely normal. One of the biggest challenges I see so many clients struggling with is learning to accept themselves. Because many of us have been told that something is wrong with us, and we need to fix ourselves. I no longer believe this. Yes, we can all improve ourselves and keep growing. But do we need fixing? I don't think so. I think this is one of the biggest lies we've been sold that so many of us feel deeply at our core. If there is something wrong with us then we are constantly on this journey to fix ourselves, and it can be a never-ending journey filled with frustration.

I encourage my clients to focus on learning to accept themselves. The good, the not so good, and everything in between.

What if we could be okay with who we are and accept ourselves exactly as we are right now?

What feeling did that bring up when you read that?

I know that may seem like a stretch to many of us because then we think it would mean that we would just be complacent about everything and no longer try to improve. I don't find that to be the case at all. I typically see that when we can accept ourselves, then we can also be more accepting of others. And we give ourselves grace to be human. Because that's what we all are. Somehow, we've bought this lie that we are supposed to be these perfect beings, instead of realizing that we are all human! We have flaws and challenges and make mistakes. It's a part of the human experience. When we accept ourselves now, we can intentionally decide how we want to move forward.

I had a client who, in the past, would describe herself as controlling. She likes things to be orderly and the way she wants them. And she could also find herself trying to control other people in her life as well. Friends and family would joke with her and tell her that she always had to be in control. So we dove into that idea. What is it in her that wants to feel control? What she came to realize is that her desire to have things planned out and organized could cross the line to wanting to control other people as well. And guess what? That never works. The only person we can control is ourselves. Because we have control over our thoughts and feelings and how we respond. She could keep getting mad when people didn't do things the way she wanted them done, or she could learn to choose her battles and decide what was most important to her. And sometimes that meant doing it herself instead of expecting someone else to do it. It also helped her to see that there is nothing wrong with wanting things done well and in a way that she prefers. But she just doesn't have to spend so much mental energy on other people and can focus it on what she wants and how she wants it.

We tend to do this, don't we? We have a certain way that we like things done and we expect others to do it the exact same way. But it usually doesn't happen that way, does it? Because everyone is unique in their own way and has their own style of doing things. My client didn't like people describing her as controlling, but she knew she could never control what they were thinking, so she shifted the thinking in her own mind. It was okay if they called her that, but she knew that she was being intentional about wanting things done well in her way. She learned to have a little more flexibility with others in the process as she accepted and gave herself grace, too.

Learning to accept ourselves for who we are and what we bring to the world can be really challenging. We've been taught that we should always criticize and never be happy with who we are. Or that we should dim our lights so that we don't outshine others. Maybe you were told that who you were was not okay. And that something was wrong with you. And you've carried that with you for your entire life.

Gay Hendricks, in the book *The Big Leap*, describes the upper limit problem as "our universal human tendency to sabotage ourselves when we have exceeded the artificial upper limit we have placed on ourselves." While accepting ourselves is the first step towards considering our upper limit thresholds, I think the four barriers he presents are helpful in showing us where many of us fall when it comes to accepting ourselves.

Hendricks describes the four barriers as:

1. The false belief that we are fundamentally flawed in some way.

2. The false belief that by succeeding, we are being disloyal to, and leaving behind, people in our past.

3. The false belief that we are a burden in the world.

4. The false belief that we must dim the bright lights of our brilliance so that we won't outshine someone in our past.

He describes these as the reasons we limit ourselves, but I also believe it is helpful in understanding why we don't learn to accept and honor ourselves for who we are. If we believe one (or more) of the false beliefs, it impacts everything we do. If I believe I am a burden in the world, I am going to do everything to prove that false belief true, even if it's subconsciously.

I personally resonate with #4 the most, as that was the conditioning I received. Don't be too big for your britches. Keep your ego in check. Don't make others feel bad by being good at something. Don't show everyone how amazing you are because then they will feel bad about themselves. Hendricks goes on to explain that for #4, people either don't shine at all, or they shine but refuse to allow themselves to experience the joy and satisfaction from it. Whoa. That one resonates with me so much.

Remember how I said that I didn't allow myself to feel my feelings most of the time? This false belief was the reason why. I knew I was good at many things, and the belief didn't stop me from doing them. But I refused to allow myself the joy and satisfaction from it because I was led to believe that it would make others uncomfortable. And it did. Understanding that hits a core wound within me and wishes that I could go back and tell myself to learn to enjoy the amazing gifts that I was given. I've learned that now and continue to work on the idea of stepping fully into my power and allowing myself to shine in a way that I know I want to shine. But it is continual work. And learning to accept myself and move towards allowing myself to be fully, unapologetically me is how I am continually moving forward.

So let me ask you a question:

What are you not accepting about yourself?

- *Is it your body?*
- *Your appearance?*
- *Your intellect?*
- *Your personality?*

- *Your intuition?*
- *The space you take up in the world?*
- *Your decisions?*
- *Your life as a whole?*

How do you feel when you don't accept yourself? Is it judgment? Contempt? Irritation? Frustration? Tap into your body and recognize what you are feeling. How is it showing up for you right now?

Take some time and journal about this.

After you've recognized the feelings and the areas where you are not accepting yourself, ask yourself what it would feel like to unapologetically accept yourself exactly as you are.

Notes

CHAPTER FOURTEEN

BELIEFS

Now that you are learning to accept yourself and tap into what makes you YOU, it's time to start doing a little more investigating into your beliefs. Beliefs are simply thoughts that you repeatedly have that feel like truths and have become a habit. Beliefs can cover a wide variety of topics. When I'm talking about beliefs, it can be anything that your mind chooses to believe. It's something that you have continually thought over and over and you have allowed to become a belief. Your beliefs might be about your values, stereotypes, cultural norms, or religious beliefs. We were not taught to question our beliefs.

In fact, most of us were told what to believe by what our parents, family, and friends believed. Their beliefs were simply passed on to us as common ideas, and we didn't even know we were allowed to question them for ourselves. For me, I was taught to listen and not to challenge any ideas or thoughts that were presented to me. I was told to accept them as truth and let them sink in and just comply. And for most of my life, I did this. I did as I was told and learned to excel in areas that led to more affirmation and praise. I was the good girl who excelled and didn't cause trouble. I believed that there was good in the world, but there was not much room for questioning.

Hard discussions and intelligent conversations are things that are not modeled well in our society. It's much easier to shame or yell or scream when someone can't see our point of view. This is what we default to when we are trained not to ask questions and decide for ourselves what we believe. Because many of us were taught that questioning meant defiance, so we simply have not learned how to be understanding of others and to seek other points of view that may not be the same as ours.

Coaching introduced me to the idea that maybe there are multiple ways you can look at something. And the idea that the way I view it is uniquely my own. And I can be okay with that. I can question beliefs that I've had for most of my life and decide, on purpose, if they are serving me or not. What an incredibly freeing revelation! I did this on my spiritual journey as well, when I decided to look at my faith as my own and really dive into what I fully believed. This has helped me allow my kids to learn to question and decide for themselves as well. Don't misunderstand and think that I am bashing educational systems or religious institutions, because I think those can be very fundamental to our growth. But those systems have not always provided much room for questioning or exploring or helping us to figure out our own answers. Which is why so many of my clients come to me not having the first clue about what their answers are. They've listened to everyone else's for most of their life and have never even considered that they might have their own answers or know what they truly want.

So learning to look at your beliefs objectively and with a new set of lenses can be incredibly helpful.

The key, again, is learning not to judge ourselves and our beliefs. When we start to uncover these beliefs and ideas that we didn't even realize we had, it can be very easy to want to judge ourselves and ask why we had never considered something different before. That's totally natural. Think of it as reexamining your beliefs. It's almost like when you declutter an area of your house. You decide what you want to keep and what you don't. That's what I suggest that you do with your beliefs. Look at them objectively and decide if it's helpful to continue to think those things.

Once you start learning to question your beliefs, it becomes so clear that there could be multiple answers and ways to look at something. I think that is such a gift to not only ourselves, but to those around us. Because then you don't get so stuck in what YOU believe that you don't consider others' points of view. Learning to question my beliefs has allowed me to open up to many other points of view that I would never have even considered.

When I was in the corporate world, I believed that climbing the corporate ladder, continuing to get promoted, and making more money were the most important things you could do. They led to status and success and continued opportunities. While I still believe some of that, I now believe that is not the only way to be successful. There are actually lots of other opportunities.

When I left the corporate world and worked for a nonprofit, I had the belief that sacrificing and serving others was a noble cause and that money wasn't as important because of all the good being done in the name of service. While I still believe that on some levels, I also no longer believe it is an either-or equation.

While growing up in a conservative Christian environment, I was led to believe that other religions are wrong. Getting involved in our local Interfaith group, where I met people from all different types of religions and faiths, has taught me that we have more in common and are typically pointing towards similar values and beliefs. We just look at them differently. And that has been an absolute gift.

Many people have beliefs about what you should or shouldn't wear. I have had these as well. As someone who is continually working on her health, I've thought there were certain things that only thin people should wear. Colored pants were one of these. I have no idea where I learned that from, but it stuck with me. I would look at people wearing brightly colored pants and thought they looked adorable, but wouldn't consider it for myself. Then one day I questioned it and ordered a pair of bright pink pants. It still took me a while to wear them, but when I did, I felt fantastic in them. And I got so many compliments. One of my favorite sayings now is "rock your pink pants!" For you, it might not be colored pants. It might be shorts, a tank top, or a sleeveless shirt. If you want to wear something, wear it and own it!

Think about some of the beliefs you have about your life.

• Do you believe that you need to have a spotless house in order to be a good mom?

• Do you believe that you have to put yourself last in order to serve your kids?

• Do you believe that being an entrepreneur has to mean only hustle and grind all the time?

• Do you believe that in order to be successful, you need a degree?

• Do you believe that you can only make a certain amount of money?

There can be endless lists of beliefs that you have that you've never questioned. So let's start with focusing on one area. It can be in your personal life, health, finances, business, or whatever you choose.

What is one belief that you have that you are not sure is helpful?

Write down your thoughts about that belief. Don't overthink it. Just go with the first thought that comes to mind. Many times we dismiss that one because we instantly tell ourselves how it's not important or it seems too big to think about. Sit with that one for a little bit. Now ask yourself if you really believe it. If you check in with your body and sit with the thought, is it something that you really believe? Write your thoughts about it.

The key to starting to question our beliefs is to know that it is okay to do so. If nobody has ever told you it's okay to question your beliefs, I'm giving you permission right now.

It is okay to question your beliefs. Read that again. It is okay to question your beliefs. It doesn't mean that you have to do anything about them. I think that's often what causes us the most turmoil. We think as soon as we look at something and question it, it means we have to fix it or change it. What if that isn't true? What if we can be super curious about it?

When I first started questioning some of my beliefs, I really had to sit with them for a while. I had to let them roll around in my mind for a little bit and see what I really thought about them. Because our old conditioning is strong. It will tell us that it's unsafe to question, especially if that was something we were told when we were younger. And sometimes we are totally okay with a belief. It serves us, and we don't need to change it. But if you take some time and think about some things you were told and encouraged to believe, I'm sure you can come up with a list of ideas to get you started on things you no longer want to believe.

Being a parent has led me to question many of the beliefs that my parents and others had about how kids should behave and what you should and shouldn't do. My kids are unique and wired very differently, and learning to understand them and adapt my parenting to help them in the best way possible has caused me to question many of the beliefs that were passed down to me. Learning to be unapologetic means questioning your beliefs, decide for yourself what you want, and then stop apologizing for it. I have done this over and over in my parenting life, as we have chosen very different school options for our son than what others believe we should. But we are the only ones who know him and know what works best for him and our family. I could keep apologizing for it, as it doesn't fit into other people's beliefs, or I could learn to own our decisions and do what's best for us, which is what I've done. I'm unapologetic about our decisions for him.

The reason we want to question beliefs is because, many times, these old beliefs are playing in our subconscious and we aren't even aware of them. Our beliefs drive our decisions and our actions without our knowledge. For example, because I was used to the corporate environment, I was used to living in the world of strategic plans and needing to have everything figured out before starting a project. The goal was to make sure that I eliminated as many risks as possible. When I decided to start my coaching business, I approached it in the same way. I thought that I needed to have everything figured out before I could move forward. As an entrepreneur, this approach is often not helpful. I found that it would keep me from taking risks and experimenting with new opportunities. This is an example of a belief that was no longer serving me. I wasn't aware of it until I learned to start to look at my beliefs objectively. Learning to understand what could potentially be holding me back and getting really honest with myself was so helpful. Because if we aren't honest about what we really believe, we can't ever decide if we actually believe it or not.

The challenge is that we don't just have beliefs, we also have many limiting beliefs. These are simply beliefs that limit us from achieving our full potential. These beliefs keep us from being unapologetic in our life and business. From living our best life and bringing all of our awesome to the world. Limiting beliefs are tricky and can hide under other thoughts because we think we "shouldn't" think them. I can't tell you how many clients will start a thought with "I know I shouldn't think this…" I often ask them who says they shouldn't think it? Do they? Or does someone else say it?

If you have never questioned your thoughts or your beliefs, I want you to give yourself some grace and a little slack. It definitely takes practice and a safe space to do so. That's what coaching has provided for me. A safe place to really process my thoughts, feelings, beliefs, and to ask myself if it is helping me. To challenge old beliefs that may have served me well in the past, but no longer apply to my life. Because you always get to decide. You are the only one who knows what is important to you and what is helpful for you. So much of the journey to being unapologetically yourself requires diving deep into the beliefs and the limiting beliefs and the thoughts that no longer serve you.

Let me ask you this:

What could be possible if you no longer believed the limiting beliefs you wrote down earlier?

Let yourself dream and consider how those beliefs might be standing in the way of the life and business you have always dreamed about.

How would it feel to release those old beliefs?

Notes

CHAPTER FIFTEEN

INTENTIONAL LIFE

After you have learned to start exploring your beliefs, now it is time to start living an intentional life. I started a podcast a few years ago called exactly that, Intentional Life. The goal is to help people learn to decide, on purpose, how they want to show up in the world, who they want to be, and create a life they love. So much of living intentionally is also living unapologetically. It's deciding who you are, what you stand for, what's important to you, and then leaning into your gifts to make it happen. The more I practiced this idea and talked about it on my weekly podcast, the more I knew that this was the missing ingredient so many of us are searching for.

We have big dreams, we have big goals, and we have ideas about how we want to impact the world. But we often do it from a place of letting life happen to us. We'll work through the obstacles and deal with the life we've been given and muscle our way through it. Do we have to do that sometimes? Absolutely! But can we also be more intentional about how we choose to show up and who we want to be in the world? YES!

Remember my friend Jamie, who was living her bucket list in her 30's? She helped me see this so clearly. She was on her third round of breast cancer and knew that she didn't have much time left. She could have intentionally decided to play it safe and to sit back and wait for her life to end. But she didn't do that. She intentionally decided to LIVE. She intentionally decided to make a bucket list and cross off as many items on it as she could. It was so inspiring to watch. It reminded me that life is short and that our intentions matter. It impacts everything we do. If we intentionally decide to be a jerk today, then we will be. If we intentionally decide to be a source of light and love, that is also our choice.

It's such a simple concept that people often overlook it. They say, "I know, I know! I can intentionally choose." But they don't really believe it. Because they are still used to letting life happen to them. They are used to just dealing with whatever comes that day. And if that's how you choose to live, then go for it! But also know that there is another option. There are millions of options available to us. Always.

The idea that we can choose how we think, which in turn creates our feelings and then drives our actions has been a life-changing concept for me.

I had heard it before, but as I mentioned earlier, Brooke Castillo from The Life Coach School simplified it in such an easy way that it truly made sense to me. I have been using it ever since I discovered her podcast in 2015. Do we have control over everything that life brings our way? Unfortunately, no. But do we always have the ability to choose how we respond, and what we think about it? Yes! There is so much power in understanding this and living this out.

Now, I know what you might be thinking. "Okay, Tammy. That all sounds great on paper and everything, but isn't that just a little too sunshine and rainbows thinking? Are you putting your head in the sand by doing this?" I don't think so. I've seen the power of this in my own life and in the lives of my coach, colleagues, and clients. When we can take our power back and intentionally decide, on purpose, how we want to think and feel, it gives us the power to live our lives unapologetically. To be emotionally and mentally healthy, and to learn to trust our intuition and our bodies. I believe we have all been given unique intuition and are continually connected to the source that created us. Some call it God, Universe, Source, Creator, or any number of identifiers. We were all created by the same creator. And we have all been given our own intuition to know what resonates with us, our bodies, and spirits. The challenge is that we have not always been taught how to tap into this. From a young age, we have actually been taught the opposite. When it is mandated that we live and behave by the rules of others and the way that traditional systems operate, it goes against many of our internal guidance indicators.

We will learn how to tap into our intuition in stronger ways when we dive into what we've been discussing in this book. Asking ourselves what we want, exploring who we are, questioning our old beliefs, and deciding, on purpose, how we want to live. Our intuition will help guide us, but it requires us to listen first. Understanding ourselves and who we are is the first step.

Learning to live intentionally is about learning to tap into that wisdom and to know that, even if it doesn't work for someone else, decisions made from our intuition and knowledge are what absolutely will work for us.

It's learning to trust that can become challenging. We have to practice, experiment, and learn to know ourselves in a way that we haven't before. For you, this might mean allowing yourself to dream. Maybe you have had desires from the time you were young, but you were never allowed to voice them. Maybe you have always wanted to try a new sport or learn to play a musical instrument, but you haven't yet taken the opportunity to do so. Maybe you have wanted to move to a foreign country or to take a month-long sabbatical to a new place. Only you know what the desires of your heart are and if you are willing to explore them.

How can you allow yourself to tap into that dream or desire you have?

We can apply intentionality to every area of our lives. With our health, our emotions, our finances, our families, our relationships, and everything in between. We don't have to allow these things to dictate our lives. We can intentionally decide how we want to approach every one of them.

Remember my son who was the picky eater? There were very few things that he wanted to eat. I could completely relate, as I was a picky eater as a child, too. I intentionally decided that dinnertime was not going to be a battle for us. I worked all day and wasn't with him, so during the time I was with him, I chose not to make this something we would continually argue about. I trusted my intuition on this one. Did other people agree with me? Definitely not. I was ridiculed and judged for not making my child eat whatever was put on his plate. But I trusted my intuition. He has since learned to like many different things. He has also learned to listen to his body and eat when he's hungry and what feels good for him. I'm still learning how to do that, as I'm continually unlearning so many old patterns of my own eating behaviors and ways that I was conditioned. Learning to intentionally decide who we want to be and what's important to us is the key to freedom. It's freedom from what others think, freedom from all the mental energy we waste on unimportant things, and freedom from whatever restricts us.

I learned to trust my intuition when I was feeling the pull to leave my corporate career. It didn't make sense to me at first, because I was doing "all the things" I thought I wanted. I had a good job, making good money, traveling the country, and continually getting promoted. So why was I feeling a pull to explore something else? Because my intuition knew there was so much more to me that I wasn't exploring.

Could I have stayed in sales for the rest of my career? Absolutely. But was it what would allow me to know myself better? Would it allow me to follow my dreams and desires of my heart? Would it allow me to help people and to share my unique gifts with the world? Probably not. For someone else, this might not be the case. They may absolutely love what they do, excel at it, and simply need to tap into their gifts in that environment more. It's different for all of us.

Intentionally deciding how to show up to our life and business is foreign to many of us, because we've been conditioned that we need others' approval or permission to do it.

This is one of the biggest things that holds my clients back. They don't always realize they're doing it, but they're waiting for permission. They're waiting for everything to be perfect. They're waiting for someone to give them a big break instead of intentionally deciding what is best for them.

We have learned to give so much of our power away to others. Teachers, coaches, bosses, mentors, and family. We give them the power to dictate how we live our lives and what we do. But it doesn't have to be that way. When you learn to accept yourself and trust your intuition, you can be free to intentionally decide everything in your life. You can decide if you want to continue to stay in the career you're in. You can decide to start enjoying your work more. You can decide if you want to start a new adventure. You can decide if you want to allow your kids to have different choices than you did. You can decide to create a business that is in total alignment with your life and looks nothing like anyone else's business. You can decide if you want to stay married or if you even want to get married. You can decide where you want to live and how you want to live. And you don't ever have to apologize for it.

I used to do this. I used to apologize for the choices and the decisions I made that were different from what others were doing, because I thought I had to. Or I thought that it wouldn't make them feel bad if I downplayed it and apologized for it. That's just simply not the case. Everything that you feel is because of what you are thinking and not because of anything someone else said or did. If you are upset because someone decides to sell everything they own and move to a remote island, that feeling of being upset is your choice. The other person is not responsible for how you feel about their decision to pack up and leave. You are responsible for your response. It's simply because of whatever thought you are thinking that's causing you to feel upset. Understanding this has changed my life. Again, not to do and say whatever I want in order to be a jerk, but to learn to listen to my body and soul and intuition and know that my choices are mine and nobody else's. My choices are my own. Your choices are your own. You get to make them. And that is freedom and taking your personal power back. That is learning to live unapologetically.

It could mean that you intentionally decide to create boundaries around a difficult family member. It might mean that you intentionally decide to start making time for yourself in the mornings before your kids wake up. It might mean that you intentionally decide who you want to spend time with. It might mean that you intentionally decide to hire a coach to help you navigate your thoughts. It might mean that you finally take that sabbatical you've been talking about for years. It might mean that you intentionally start paying attention to where you buy items and how they are sourced. It might mean that you intentionally decide to start living your life and no longer allow fear to keep you from taking a step towards your dream. I don't know what it means for you, but you do. You know what being more intentional would mean for you.

An intentional life begins with deciding ahead of time. Deciding what you want, who you want to be in the world, and what is important to you. It's available to all of us.

I want you to take a minute and think about why you picked up this book. You might have picked it up because you know me, have followed me on social media, or simply because it looked interesting. Here are a few questions to consider.

What intrigued you about the title?

What has been resonating with you so far?

Is there an area in your life where you want to be more unapologetic?

Think about what that is and write your thoughts in the space below or in your journal. Living unapologetically is completely possible for you. Will it take some work? Absolutely. Will you have bumps in the road? Most likely. But will it be worth it to continue to move towards who you are at your core and what feels like absolute truth to you? Definitely!!

Notes

CHAPTER SIXTEEN

WHAT NOW?

So we've talked about why we apologize, how to interrupt our patterns, finding what works for you, being curious, focusing on your mindset, learning to experiment, accepting ourselves, questioning beliefs, and learning to lead an intentional life. WHEW! I'm so glad you're still here and reading. Thank you for taking the time to do something for you. It's so important.

But I don't want you to just read this book and say that it was helpful. I would love for you to implement something you learned. If you're ready and want to start living more unapologetically, then I want you to decide right now which one of those areas you are going to focus on this week. Go ahead and write it down here.

I went through so many stages of consuming information and taking all the courses and reading all the books, so I totally get it. It's easy to stay stuck in the consumption or student mode. But challenging yourself to actually implement or focus on ONE thing from this book is a great first step. And I would love to hear from you and help encourage you. Connect with me on social media channels shown in the back of this book.

I also want to warn you. As you start looking at many of the ideas and concepts I've presented in this book and start to work on them, you will face some roadblocks. It's totally normal. So please don't freak out. Just when you think you are making some progress, life may happen. Kids get sick, aging parent issues come up, business challenges happen, or anything in between. This happens to all of us. It's why this is a journey and not a destination. So many of the concepts I present are still areas that I continue to work on. Some are more prevalent than others, but we often have so much conditioning and unlearning to experience that it will take layers and multiple times of looking at the same issues before we feel like we've moved past them. That is where a great coach can be incredibly helpful. Having someone to help us see our thinking when we can't has been some of the most healing and powerful work I have done in my life. Of course, I know a fantastic coach who just happened to write this book. But I also know a large variety of coaches who can help you.

You may also feel some guilt as you start on this journey. Guilt for not recognizing some of these things sooner, guilt for working on yourself when everyone has always told you not to, or guilt for how long it takes to work through some of these things. Again, know that this is common. Just remember that you are feeling guilt simply because of a thought you are thinking.

If you are thinking "I am spending too much time working on myself" then you may feel guilty. Just get curious about that and ask yourself if that is a helpful thought for you.

And remember that you always get to decide how you want to feel.

There are so many feelings that may come up as you start to do this work. Frustration, questions, uneasiness, fear. These are all common. Because most of us have never taken the time to work on ourselves and get really honest without judgment. Some of you may need to forgive yourself for past mistakes that you have been beating yourself up about. This book may have brought some of that up for you. Just know that you are totally safe and trust that working on yourself is always a helpful endeavor.

And if you are an entrepreneur, it's why I created the Intentional Entrepreneur membership. Having a coach to help guide you through the ups and downs of entrepreneurship along with others in similar shoes is incredibly helpful to keep you moving forward and knowing you are not alone. It also helps us continue to grow and evolve together in community, which is a beautiful thing. If you're interested in learning more, you can find the link in the resources section.

I have also included some of the tools and resources that have been helpful for me on this journey in that section. Feel free to check them out, but also realize that we all learn differently and in our own ways. What worked for me may not work for you and that is totally okay. I'd also love to hear if you have helpful resources that you've used on your journey, as sharing ideas and helpful thoughts is so important on our journey to living unapologetically.

Now I want to take you back to the beginning of this book. Do you remember these questions?

• If you were unapologetic, what would be different in your life?

• How would you show up differently?

• What would being unapologetic mean to you?

• Are your answers different? Or the same? Take a minute and compare them.

I want to remind you that while I have loved writing this book and sharing my story and experiences that I've had, I do not have your answers. I can help guide you and prompt you, but only YOU have your answers. You are the only one who knows what living unapologetically would mean to you. You are the only one who knows where your work is. There is help if you need it, but this is your work to do. I know when I say that, it can seem overwhelming and may cause some anxiety. But it doesn't have to. Remember, there are coaches (like me) and guides and teachers who are always available to help guide you. You just have to be willing to take a step and ask for help. So, let me ask you:

What if you looked at your journey to being unapologetic as an adventure?

This thought has helped me so much. Learning about myself and understanding myself in a deeper way has been a continual adventure. It's full of ups and downs and epiphanies and challenging moments. But it has been so worth it. I am continually learning to move towards living unapologetically in so many areas of my life, and you can too.

Learning to live unapologetically matters because it allows us to stand in our power. It allows us to bring our gifts to the world. It allows us to make space for others to also live unapologetically too. The ripple effect of you living unapologetically will go far beyond just you. And that is a beautiful gift to yourself and to the world.

Thank you for continuing to show up for YOU. I wrote this book for you and for everyone who knows they have something awesome to bring to the world, but continue to apologize for who they are and what they want.

What if that stopped today?

What if you intentionally decided to be unapologetic?

I believe in you!

Unapologetic Tammy

Notes

RESOURCES PAGE

Here are the books and articles mentioned in this book.

1. *How to Do the Work* - Dr. Nicole LePera

3. *Much Love from Jamie* - Jamie Barkes Pursley

4. *Mental Vitamins* - Dr. Rick Ridnour

5. *Becoming a Lifechanger* - Tammy Helfrich

6. "Dualistic Thinking article for CAC 2017" - Richard Rohr

7. *What to Expect When You're Expecting* - Heidi Murkoff

8. *The Road Back to You* - Ian Cron

9. *The Body Keeps the Score* - Bessel van der Kolk M.D.

10. *The Gifts of Imperfection* - Brene Brown

11. *The Big Leap* - Gay Hendricks

NEXT STEPS

There are multiple ways you can dive into this work more.

My podcast, *Intentional Life*, is available on all podcast apps. I talk about creating a life intentionally, which allows you to live as an unapologetic you.

I also work directly with coaching clients to dive deeper into who you are and who you want to become. Together, we discover old thoughts and patterns that are keeping you from being fully you and intentionally taking steps towards being more unapologetic.

I love hearing from people who are continuing to grow and evolve and become more fully themselves. You can also connect with me on Facebook (@tammyhelfrichblog), Instagram (@tammyhelfrichcoaching), or on my website (www.tammyhelfrich.com).

ABOUT THE AUTHOR

 Tammy Helfrich is a Life & Business Mindset coach and the host of the Intentional Life podcast. She is passionate about helping people live unapologetically as who they were created to be.

She lives in IL with her husband, two teenage sons, and their handsome but devious Silver Labrador, Steel. She truly believes that we can all create a life we absolutely love, simply by learning to understand, accept, and honor ourselves. When we do this, we give ourselves the permission to be fully us, which allows others to be fully themselves as well. In turn, that not only changes our immediate family and neighborhoods, but starts a ripple effect that impacts our world.

When she's not coaching, writing, or podcasting, you can often find her in nature, grounding in the beauty of this earth, or dreaming about her next adventure. She believes that we can truly impact the world around us by embracing our unique nature and unapologetically living our best life. You can learn more about Tammy on her website, www.tammyhelfrich.com.

ACKNOWLEDGEMENTS

I am so grateful for the team that helped Unapologetic come to life. Special thanks to my writing coach, Jim Woods, for his continual support and encouragement to finish this book. My editor, TK Johnson, was so helpful and great to work with. Sarah Cervantes from Seven Brighter Design took my cover concepts and brought them to life perfectly. When they say it takes a village to write a book, they are not kidding!

Thank you to everyone who read pre-release copies and offered feedback and endorsements. I am grateful for your time and support.

I feel fortunate to have an amazing group of family, friends and community around me who support and encourage me to be unapologetically me. Thank you for investing in me and showing me love and encouragement always.

And thank you for reading this book. I hope it will help you take steps towards being unapologetically you. I look forward to hearing all about it!

Made in the USA
Monee, IL
16 August 2021